Black Hollywood

FROM 1970 TO TODAY

BLACK HOLLYWOOD

FROM 1970 TO TODAY

by Gary Null

A CITADEL PRESS BOOK

Published by Carol Publishing Group

ACKNOWLEDGMENTS

Special thanks to Eileen Davis and Trudy Golubic, without whose editorial assistance this manuscript would not have been published for another year. Additional thanks to Charles Woods, who spent countless hours showing me rare vintage footage from his private collection.

A Citadel Press Book
Published by Carol Publishing Group

Citadel Press is a registered trademark of Carol Communications, Inc.
Editorial Offices: 600 Madison Avenue, New York, N.Y. 10022
Sales and Distribution Offices: 120 Enterprise Avenue, Secaucus, N.J. 07094
In Canada: Canadian Manda Group, P.O. Box 920, Station U, Toronto, Ontario M8Z 5P9
Queries regarding rights and permissions should be addressed to Carol Publishing Group, 600 Madison Avenue, New York, N.Y. 10022

Carol Publishing Group books are available at special discounts for bulk purchases, for sales promotions, fund-raising, or educational purposes. Special editions can be created to specifications. For details, contact Special Sales Department, Carol Publishing Group, 120 Enterprise Avenue, Secaucus, N.J. 07094

Designer: A. Christopher Simon

Manufactured in the United States of America
10 9 8 7 6 5 4 3 2 1

LIBRARY OF CONGRESS CATALOGING-IN-PUBLICATION DATA

Null, Gary.
    Black Hollywood : from 1970 to today / by Gary Null.
        p. cm.
    "A Citadel Press book."
    ISBN 0-8065-1216-4 (paper) :
    1. Afro-Americans in motion pictures. 2. Afro-American motion picture actors and actresses. I. Title.
PN1995.9.N4N79 1993
791.43'6520396073—dc20   92-37551
                                                     CIP

Soapdish (1991): Whoopi Goldberg

CONTENTS

Black Hollywood

FROM 1970 TO TODAY

Birth of a Nation (1915): Walter Long as Gus

Introduction

The 1990s opened with a promise of booming opportunity for black artists. The signal success of stars such as Eddie Murphy, Oprah Winfrey, and Arsenio Hall in the eighties created unbridled enthusiasm at the start of the new decade. The media put the message out early in 1990: "Black Is Hot," "Black Is In," and perhaps most important to the Hollywood establishment, "Black means money—and lots of it." On March 4, both the front page of the *New York Times* entertainment section and the pink pages of the *San Francisco Chronicle* gave lengthy reviews to *House Party*, a low-budget black teen comedy that eventually drew more than $26 million at the box office. A few days later, the *Wall Street Journal* followed suit.[1]

The reviews didn't merely critique the film, how- ever. They heralded a new era for black filmmakers. The *Times* article, "In Hollywood, Black Is In," opened by describing the difficulties black artists have faced in the past. "Would the same thing happen in 1990 to a black filmmaker who came knocking on Hollywood's door?" it asks. "Not likely, for a number of reasons, most of them economic. Black filmmakers are being welcomed into the film industry as never before. Just about every studio in town has a project in development with a black director . . . or wants to."[2]

The *San Francisco Chronicle* noted that Reginald and Warrington Hudlin, who wrote, produced and directed *House Party*, "are crossing the threshold into mainstream moviemaking to contribute to the new wave of black-experience films considered a positive trend in Hollywood."[3] By mid-1991, that wave had reached huge proportions. Four new films by black directors were released by the summer, casting up-and-coming talents Mario Van Peebles, John Singleton, and Matty Rich into the spotlight along with the irrev-

[1]Wynter, Leon E., "Selling Black Films to a Wider Audience," *Wall Street Journal*, March 9, 1990, p. 81.

[2]Greenberg, James, "In Hollywood, Black Is In," *New York Times*, March 4, 1990, section 2, p. 1.

[3]Stanley, John, "Black Teen Tales Making for Mainstream," *Datebook, San Francisco Chronicle*, March 4, 1990, p. 23.

The Mask of Fu Manchu (1932): Blacks as ceremonial warriors

erent Spike Lee, an independent filmmaker who first sidestepped Hollywood's apathy toward black films with *She's Gotta Have It* in 1986.

So where does that leave things? Hollywood has long been criticized for its prejudicial treatment of blacks. But have the achievements of people like Eddie Murphy, and now the new wave of black directors, finally exorcized the specter of racism in Hollywood once and for all? Quite possibly. Certainly we are seeing more blacks in the industry—both behind and in front of the camera. In 1989, we also saw the release of *Glory* and *Driving Miss Daisy*, both exceptionally fine films which provided quality roles for black actors (particularly Morgan Freeman who starred in both, and Denzel Washington, who won the Oscar for *Glory*). The movies released in 1991, for their part, featured excellent acting from fresh faces and skilled production work from talented people behind the scenes.

With the success of these new films, we appear to be in the midst of a "black renaissance" in which the flourishing of black talent will be sustained for many years to come. As the *Times* article pointed out. "Hollywood has long recognized the potency of the black film-going audience. . . . The crucial difference now is that industry marketing mavens long resistant to the idea are beginning to recognize that a white audience will spend money to see black movies."[4] Thus it is entirely possible that a critical mass acceptance has finally been achieved and that backsliding will be prevented by the sheer number of working black filmmakers and performers and the clout they wield.

On the other hand, it must be noted that Hollywood, much like the American viewing public, is notoriously fickle. What's in today may very well be out tomorrow. From Hollywood's perspective, the determining factor in the success of any one film or actor is the profit to be made. The idealistic concept of supporting minority efforts remains a low priority, unless there's money in the process. In the scramble for the all-important buck, even talent and creative ability are of secondary importance. If a particular film generates a profit and also happens to reflect favorably upon an ethnic

[4]Greenberg, *supra.*

12

The Emperor Jones (1933): Paul Robeson

group, then so be it. But the latter is a tangential benefit, not a motivating factor.

Today, Hollywood is backing black filmmakers and actors because of their rise in popularity and, hence, profitability. Unlike the thirties and forties when superstars such as Bette Davis, Greta Garbo, and Clark Gable enjoyed long and sustained careers, today's movie stars have a much more ephemeral notoriety. The public has a short attention span, and actors rarely maintain star status for more than four or five years. With a few exceptions, the same principle holds true for film genres. Sidney Poitier, Bill Cosby, and Danny Glover are exceptions of course.

The pendulum of interest swings back and forth, taking certain types of movies in and out of favor. Rosalind Cash, for one, recalls how her career slowed considerably in the late 1970s. "I saw a lot of films being made in the early seventies, and then it seemed to suddenly end. This paralleled my own experience. I had quite a bit of work in the mid-seventies, and then it seemed to come to an abrupt halt. I remember my agent saying, not facetiously, that blacks were out of style. I was angered by that. I wondered how a whole group of people who helped build this country could suddenly be out of style. We are more than a fad. My agent simply replied that the era was coming for blue-eyed blondes."[5]

It may appear that Hollywood executives hold all the cards in determining the fate of black filmmakers and actors, but that is not necessarily the case. Certainly, the vast machinery that regulates the distribution of films and public relations plays a substantial role in determining which films and actors will succeed or fail. The decisions as to who gets the distribution and public relations

---

[5]Interview with Rosalind Cash by Gary Null, November 13, 1989.

Judge Priest (1934): Hattie McDaniel and Ben Carter

dollars remain in the hands of studio executives. But what influences those decisions in the first place? While personal preference and the old-boy network both play their part, money has become the largest motivation by far. In today's marketplace, any performer, film genre, or ethnic group that proves to be profitable will receive support.

In most cases, personal likes and dislikes do not even enter into the equation. Undoubtedly, there are many studio bigwigs who do not like Eddie Murphy; and it doesn't matter whether their distaste stems from his type of humor or his race. Murphy has been a proven moneymaker, and these individuals are in business. Given a chance to sign Murphy to a contract, most of the very people who dislike him would do so without a moment's hesitation. What counts is the bottom line. Will the film make money? Will the artist be a box office draw? If the answer to these questions is yes, then just about anything goes.

In the end, the buying public plays the largest role in determining profitability and success, followed to a lesser degree by the artist him- or herself.[6] It was the public, not the studios, that first recognized comedians such as Murphy and Richard Pryor. Once these performers' popularity was irrefutable, the studios jumped on the bandwagon. The same pattern has since occurred with the black independent filmmakers, with Spike Lee serving as a prime example. (How may studio executives other than Warner Bros. are now kicking themselves for not having signed him on when they had the chance?)

More important, Lee's success proved Hollywood is sorely out of touch with what is hot. After all, Lee's popularity did not come from studio executives with the insight to recognize creative talent and measure its popular appeal. Rather, it came from the public's acceptance and acclaim for *Do the Right Thing*. Often, success is a "chicken and egg" situation—what is the cause and what is the effect? But the compelling point to be made about film in the eighties and nineties is that a shift of power took place, moving the controlling influence from the studios to the public and the artists.

Show Boat (1936): Paul Robeson

---

[6]We qualify the importance of the individual artist because so many actors of extraordinary talent have never enjoyed wide popular acclaim. The reasons for this will be discussed throughout the book, but we make no pretense about being able to offer a definitive answer. In some cases, an actor's success may be based solely on connections. Perhaps Ms. Such-and-Such is the daughter of a famous actress; perhaps Mr. So-and-So slept with the right person. Then again, a performer's success may be attributed to timing. Everything was right about Sidney Poitier—he was born at the right time, with the right type of talent and somehow came upon the right form of expression at a time when the public was ready to accept exactly what he had to offer. Paul Robeson's talent, on the other hand, was never fully appreciated in the thirties and forties. Would the outcome be any different if Robeson were born today? Conversely, how would Eddie Murphy have fared had he been born fifty years earlier? Beyond that, a performer's determination, luck, and even "karma" may play a role in his or her success.

Belle of the Nineties (1934): Libby Taylor with Mae West

1
An Historical Perspective

Filmmaking has been highly prejudicial to black people since "actuality" films were first introduced by Thomas Edison in the early 1900s, says Thomas Cripps, a cinema historian and author. "Wherever you looked, there was an attempt to get film that might be called 'anthropology,' although it was hardly scientific. Blacks were on film as part of the normal course of looking for the exotic. This also suggests what people thought of as black in the larger context of society. In other words, nobody thought of them as ordinary folks. They were always on the periphery of white life; they lived down South somewhere or in a corner of the white world."

According to Cripps, a typical example of actuality footage would show blacks participating in a watermelon-eating contest. "Obviously, it is part of the stereotype we all know: 'Blacks like watermelon,' " he says. But on the other hand, films

were not edited in those early days. Consequently, some footage of blacks was an accurate and dignified portrayal of their lives. As an example, Cripps points to Edison's film of the Ninth and Tenth Cavalry returning from Cuba.

"Now you couldn't put funny hats on the blacks; you couldn't hand them watermelons. When you saw those soldiers, they were black soldiers, there in their formations, on their horses. So in the early days of film, blacks were both exactly the way whites wanted them to be, and also exactly as blacks would have proudly wished to be—as soldiers."

The advent of film editing, says Cripps, was "the beginning of the end for blacks" because it allowed the more accurate portrayals to be cut.[7] But he and most other black film historians agree that the real death knell for black dignity was sounded by D.W. Griffith's *The Birth of a Nation* in 1915. "The movie was technologically superior and ahead of its time, but as it relates to the black image, it set the tone for many years to come," sociologist Charles

---

[7]Interview with Thomas Cripps (author of *Slow to Fade* and *Black Film as Genre*) by Tony Brown, on "Tony Brown's Journal",

Green Pastures (1936): George Reed as Sunday schoolteacher Mr. Deshee

Green Pastures 1936: James Fuller as Cain the Sixth, Eddie "Rochester" Anderson as Noah (seated), and Frank Wilson as Moses

Woods says. "All of your stereotyped characters were present in *The Birth of a Nation*. D.W. Griffith gave us the black buck, the mammy, the coon—all of the images were there. The film, set during the Civil War, showed blacks in such a poor light that it glorified the formation of the Klan."[8]

Author Donald Bogle concurs: "In almost every way, *The Birth of a Nation* was a stupendous undertaking, unlike any film that had preceded it. . . . [The film], however, not only vividly re-created history, but revealed its director's philosophical concept of the universe and his personal racial bigotry."[9]

"The war years take their toll," writes Bogle. "In Piedmont, the Cameron family is terrorized by a troop of Negro raiders, and all the South undergoes 'ruin, devastation, rape, and pillage.' Then comes the Reconstruction. Carpetbaggers and uppity niggers from the North move into Piedmont, exploiting and corrupting the former slaves, unleashing the sadism and bestiality innate in the

Our Gang in *Night'n Gales* (1937): Buckwheat (William Henry Thomas Jr.) with (from left) Spanky McFarland, Carl "Alfalfa" Switzer, and Eugene "Porky" Lee

---

[8]Interview with Charles Woods by Gary Null, March 1, 1990.
[9]Bogle, Donald, *Toms, Coons, Mulattoes, Mammies & Bucks*, New York: Continuum, 1973, p. 10.

Jezebel (1938): Eddie "Rochester" Anderson and Stymie Beard with Bette Davis and Fay Bainter

Negro, turning the once congenial darkies into renegades and using them to 'crush the white South under the heel of the black South.'"

Griffith's concept of the universe centered around maintaining the status quo. The pre-Civil War South stood for order, one in which both blacks and whites knew their place. The war shattered this order and created chaos. Hence, Griffith presents an obviously biased and racist view of blacks. The only "darkies" who do not look like villains are the dark-skinned blacks who know their place. The stereotypes he created would persist in the American theater for many years to come.

Harlem on the Prairie (1938): Mantan Moreland and Spencer Williams Jr.

The Thief of Bagdad (1940): Rex Ingram as Djinni

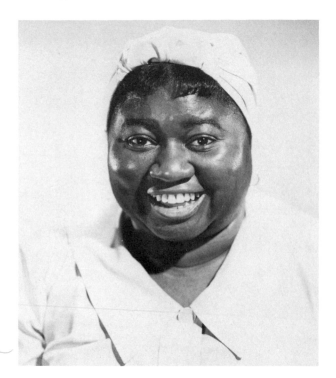

Maryland (1940): Hattie McDaniel

Belle Starr (1941): Louise Beavers with John Shepperd (later Shepperd Strudwick)

Two Sisters and a Sailor (1945): Lena Horne, accompanied by Olinette Miller, Phil Moore (piano), and Aaron Walker

Cabin in the Sky (1943): Eddie "Rochester" Anderson and Lena Horne

Tales of Manhattan (1942): Ethel Waters

Family Honeymoon (1948): Hattie McDaniel with Claudette
Colbert

2
Getting a Foot in the Door —A Forty Year Ordeal

In the thirties and forties, the persistent stereotypes severely limited some uniquely talented black performers, such as Paul Robeson, Ethel Waters, and Hattie McDaniel, who rarely received roles outside of the established norm.[10] They could play slaves, maids, comics, or musicians, but not the meaningful, dramatic characters their white counterparts received. As a result, the work of many talented black performers went unnoticed.

Lorenzo Tucker, handsome and gifted actor, acquired his fame as the "Black Valentino." He was the protégé of Oscar Micheaux, an independent film producer. Had Tucker not been black, the major studios almost certainly would have been eager to sign him up and profit from his reputation. Lena Horne's talent, on the other hand, made her the black sweetheart of the 1940s (except to movie exhibitors in the South). Few will deny that her acceptance by white audiences had much to do with her light skin and delicate features. In praising her beauty, critics referred to Horne as "copper colored" or "cafe au lait," not as "black" or "Negroid."

In the 1950s, Sidney Poitier broke new ground by playing characters of substance, even in his debut performance in *No Way Out*. Poitier shattered the stereotypes in virtually every character he portrayed. By the early 1970s, Poitier was so popular that he broke yet another barrier: He was one of the first black actors to become a box office draw. But Poitier and Harry Belafonte would remain the exceptions to the rule until comedians such as Eddie Murphy and Richard Pryor achieved fame in the 1980s.

---

[10]Robeson's performance in *The Emperor Jones* (1933) serves as an isolated exception. Robeson plays an escaped prisoner who later becomes the leader of a small Caribbean island. Although the film represented the first time a black actor played a strong central character in an interracial cast, it still had its limitations. Film historian Charles Woods notes that a scene in which Robeson kills his white prison guard was edited out, even though it was originally shot in its entirety. The idea of a black man killing a white man, even on the screen, was utterly taboo.

No Way Out (1950): Frederick O'Neal

Odds Against Tomorrow (1959): Harry Belafonte with Ed Begley and Robert Ryan

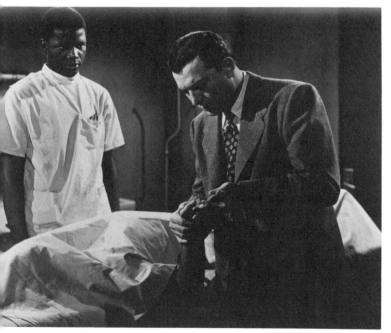

⚓ *No Way Out* (1950): Sidney Poitier with Stephen McNally

Native Son (1951): Richard Wright (the author) and Gloria Madison

Edge of the City (1957): Sidney Poitier with John Cassavetes

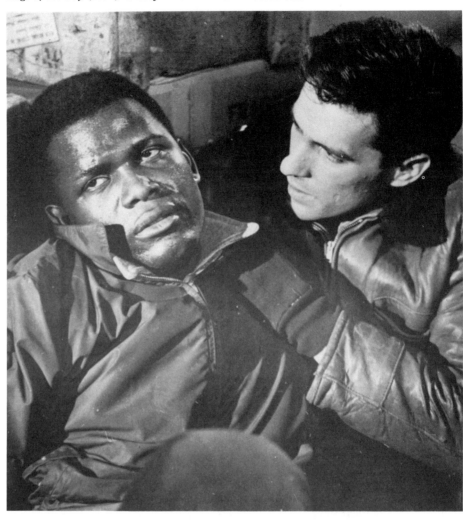

Goodbye, My Lady (1956): Sidney Poitier with Brandon de Wilde

25

The Defiant Ones (1958): Sidney Poitier with Tony Curtis

A Raisin in the Sun (1961): Claudia McNeil and Sidney Poitier

Imitation of Life (1959): Juanita Moore

26

Pressure Point (1962): Sidney Poitier with Bobby Darin

Nothing But a Man (1964): Ivan Dixon and Abbey Lincoln

In the Heat of the Night (1967): Sidney Poitier with Rod Steiger

 Guess Who's Coming to Dinner (1967): Roy Glenn Sr., Beah Richards, and Sidney Poitier

The Biggest Bundle of Them All (1968): Godfrey Cambridge

The Split (1968): Jim Brown with Julie Harris

Salt and Pepper (1968): Sammy Davis Jr. with Peter Lawford

Uptight (1968): Ruby Dee and Ossie Davis

If He Hollers, Let Him Go! (1968): Raymond St. Jacques

29

Black Girl (1969): Peggy Pettitt

Riot (1969): Jim Brown with Ben Carruthers

In the meantime, black artists could give memorable and even stellar performances but still not gain true success. Afterwards, it was if they had simply disappeared. Take Cicely Tyson, who gave brilliant performances in *Sounder* on the big screen and *The Autobiography of Miss Jane Pittman* and *A Woman Called Moses* on TV. Tyson is certainly as talented as actresses such as Meryl Streep and Glenn Close, for example, both of whom have achieved far greater stardom. As a result, it is difficult not to figure racism into the equation in comparing their careers.

More recently, Louis Gossett Jr. faced the same obstacle in building his career. In 1982, Gossett won an Oscar for his role as the tough drill instruc-

The Lost Man (1969): Sidney Poitier with Joanna Shimkus

tor, Sgt. Foley, in *An Officer and a Gentleman*. But Hollywood barely responded, except with action films like *Iron Eagle I, II* and *III*. Rather than launching a brilliant career, Gossett was left feeling disillusioned. "I expected this pie in the sky," he says. "I pictured every studio calling me. I expected the world—and nobody called." Gossett went through a tumultuous period in which he "could not see light at the end of the tunnel."

100 Rifles (1969): Jim Brown with Burt Reynolds and Raquel Welch

Black Journal (TV, 1969): From left: Shawn Walker, Tony Batten, executive producer William Greaves, Kent Garrett, and St. Claire Bourne

31

Cottom Comes to Harlem (1970): Raymond St. Jacques

One More Time (1970): Sammy Davis Jr. with Peter Lawford

Halls of Anger (1970): Calvin Lockhart and James A. Watson Jr.

The McMasters (1970): Brock Peters with Burl Ives

... *tick* ... *tick* ... *tick* (1970): Jim Brown with Fredric March and George Kennedy

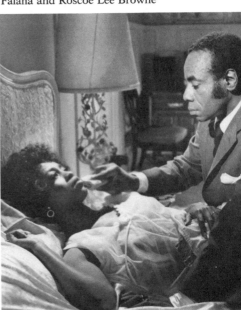

The Liberation of L. B. Jones (1970): Lola Falana and Roscoe Lee Browne

You've Got to Walk It Like You Talk It (1971): Richard Pryor

They Call Me MISTER Tibbs (1970): Beverly Todd and Sidney Poitier

33

Black Jesus (1970): Woody Strode

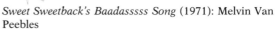

Skin Game (1971): Louis Gossett Jr. with James Garner

34

Shaft (1971): Richard Roundtree

Melinda (1972): Rosalind Cash and Calvin Lockhart with Paul Stevens

The Legend of Nigger Charley (1972): Fred Williamson

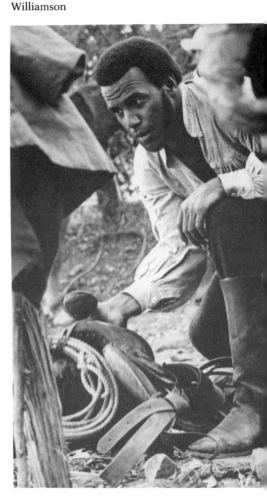

Hammer (1972): Fred Williamson

Remarkably, he managed to overcome the disappointment and bitterness and has since gotten back on his feet. "Here I am again, ready to make my particular artistic statement," he says.

Even more remarkable is Gossett's ability to look beyond the racism that has caused such grief for him and many others. He believes that black performers must persist in overcoming the obstacles. "When a white writer and white producer get together to do a script, they think in terms of white—that's the way they were raised, that's who they are, that's who they see in the mirror every day," he says. "It takes an extra effort for them to say, 'Well maybe Sidney Poitier can play this part.' That's outside their circle. That is a natural thing. When we wake up, we think in terms of black. That is a residual thing across the country, because we

Black Gunn (1972): Jim Brown and Brenda Sykes

Cool Breeze (1972): From left: Jim Watkins, Thalmus Rasulala, and Lincoln Kilpatrick

Slaughter (1972): Jim Brown with Cameron Mitchell

are still growing, but we still think in terms of us and them. . . . Hopefully, with enough prayer, we will mix that up eventually, . . . but that is not yet."

Gossett expresses an opinion that has gained favor among black actors and actresses. Rather than focus on the limitations imposed by Hollywood, these performers are concentrating on their own power to effect change. "So many generations have been saying, 'Boy, it's so hard for me to get out from under here. I am just going to do the best I can right here,'" Gossett notes. "That has to be replaced with, 'I can do anything, regardless of whether I have money or not, anything I dream.'"[11]

Comedian and actress Whoopi Goldberg has put that philosophy to use with substantial results. She gained critical recognition for her portrayal of Celie in *The Color Purple* and later would win an Oscar for her role in *Ghost*. As a black woman some perceived to be short on both sex appeal and glamour, Goldberg has faced many possible career

[11]"The Story of a People: The Black Road to Hollywood," one-hour television special hosted by Sheryl Lee Ralph, 1990

Lady Sings the Blues (1972): Billy Dee Williams

The Limit (1972):
Yaphet Kotto with
Ted Cassidy (left)

Top of the Heap (1972): Beatrice Webster and Christopher
St. John

Trouble Man (1972): Robert Hooks with Wayne
Storm

Charley One-Eye (1972): Richard Roundtree

limitations. But she doesn't let that stop her from pursuing her craft.

"I see no limitations for myself. This is why I don't let anyone refer to me as a black actor," she says. "I am not going to let anybody tell me what I can and cannot do . . . I am not going to let them tell me, 'Hey, this isn't written for you.' Damn straight it is. You may not want me, but you are not going to tell me it was not written for me. What experiences are there in this film that I could not have lived?"

She believes that movies like *The Color Purple* deliver a message with wide appeal. "This is horse manure when people say, 'Only this kind of person will know this experience.' You know, white people get oppressed, women get oppressed, Jews get oppressed. Anyone who has lived among a people who have been oppressed will understand the message of the film," she says. "*The Color Purple* was not about white people keeping black people down. It was about a man keeping a woman down. It didn't matter what color they were. So it didn't matter to me that Steven Spielberg wanted to do it. Nobody else wanted to make *The Color Purple*.

Man and Boy (1972): Bill Cosby with Dub Taylor and Henry Silva

39

Superfly (1972): Gloria Frazier and Ron O'Neal

Hit Man (1972): Bernie Casey

Nobody wanted to touch it. Black filmmakers didn't want to deal with it. I understand that people in Idaho may not be ready for lesbian relationships on a screen, that they may not have been ready for black actors. But they took to us; took to the movie. That's right. That is the right thing—for people to take to something and say, 'Yes, this is part of me.'"[12]

To work on *The Color Purple*, Spielberg had the inestimable help of Quincy Jones as coproducer.

[12]*Id.*

Black Mama, White Mama (1972): Pam Grier with Margaret Markov

Hickey and Boggs (1972): Bill Cosby with Robert Culp

Across 110th Street (1972): Yaphet Kotto with Anthony Quinn

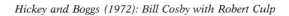

The Thing With Two Heads (1972): Rosey Grier with Ray Milland

Blacula (1972): Vonetta McGee and William Marshall

41

Sanford and Son (TV, 1972–77): Redd Foxx and Demond Wilson

3
The Business of Making Films

The nature of Hollywood has changed tremendously in the last twenty years. As films became increasingly more expensive to produce, the studios turned their attention almost solely to the bottom line. Movies get made—and performers make it big—when industry executives believe they can generate substantial profits. Indeed, the people who make films have power as long as they make the right decisions; they lose their jobs if they consistently make the wrong ones. Within this structure, the idea of supporting minority efforts takes a back seat to the process of making money. Movies such as *The Autobiography of Miss Jane Pittman,* * *Glory,* and *A Soldier's Story* are made if they show clear profit potential.

Over the years, the single-minded focus on money has been fueled by a fundamental shift of power in the industry. Before the 1960s, each studio had one or two top men (such as Sam Goldwyn) who had the final word on what movies

*(made for television)

would be made and who would star in them. Actors and actresses generally were under contract to one studio or another, and when a film was to be made, the studio simply chose a performer from among its pool.

Today, that paternalistic structure is long gone. Films have become packaged "deals" that get made with the input of many people. Among the most powerful of these dealmakers are the agents who represent actors, directors, writers, and nearly everyone else down the line. They now wield as much power as the studio heads of yesteryear because they control these clients. The agents exist solely to make money for their clients and themselves (and not necessarily in that order) by maximizing salaries and, hopefully, participation deals.

The shift from studio contract to agent representation may be one of the single most important factors in the exorbitant rise in filmmaking costs. Studios can easily pay millions of dollars to get a dynamic director for a single film. Francis Ford

A Warm December (1972): Sidney Poitier and Esther Anderson

Coppola, for instance, reportedly commanded some $3 million for *The Godfather III*. By the time these salaries have been paid, costs can soar beyond $10 million even before the film is shot. As a result, the average movie today costs in excess of $15 million, while some of the finest films of Hollywood's Golden Age cost only $2 to $3 million.

The superstar syndrome affects the entire structure of Hollywood. There is only so much money to go around, and the large-scale, star-studded movies take away from the production and promotion of smaller films. (Indeed, Orion Pictures, which found itself with the Best Picture of the Year in both 1990 and 1991 and still went into Chapter 11 shortly thereafter.) In addition, a studio's willingness to take a chance decreases in direct proportion to the rising costs. Rather than stick their necks out for a new talent or an unusual film, the studios will put big bucks behind a proven success or the superstar of the day. As a result, many sequel films are made to capitalize on the original formula.

Only a handful of superstars can "create" a deal at any given time, however, before their preferred status wanes. Burt Reynolds was enormously popular in the late 1970s and early 1980s, for example, but people grew tired of him by the end of the decade. After a few flops, he was mingling among

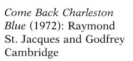

Come Back Charleston Blue (1972): Raymond St. Jacques and Godfrey Cambridge

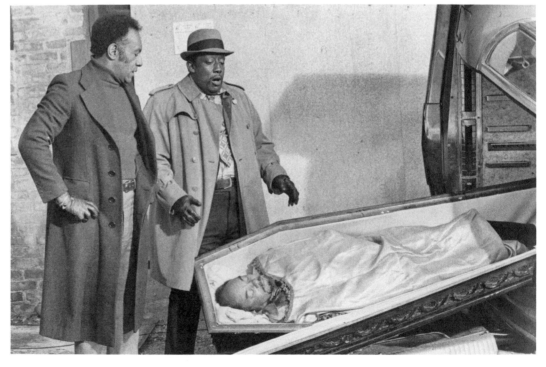

The Mack (1973): Max
Julien and Richard Pryor

Sammy Davis Jr. in the
early 1970s

Superfly T.N.T. (1973): Sheila Frazier and
Ron O'Neal

Maurie (1973): Janet MacLachlan and Bernie Casey

Scream, Blacula, Scream (1973): Pam Grier and William Marshall

Hit (1973): Billy Dee Williams with Warren Kemmerling

Book of Numbers (1973): Freyda Payne and Phillip Michael Thomas

Live and Let Die (1973): Geoffrey Holder with Jane Seymour

Gordon's War (1973): From left: David Downing, Paul Winfield, Tony E. King, and Carl Lee

the menials like everyone else. Richard Pryor's career followed the same pattern. He shot to the top, gained tremendous power, and then slumped after a few box office flops.

While Eddie Murphy has been riding the crest of success, he too shows every sign of losing his appeal. Following the *Beverly Hills* films and other box office hits, Murphy's latest endeavors have not been critical and financial successes including *Eddie Murphy Raw, Golden Child, Another 48 Hrs.,* and *Harlem Nights.* In the nineties, *Boomerang* did well enough and, later, *The Distinguished Gentleman* struck box-office gold. Meanwhile, few black actors other than Murphy and Pryor and Danny Glover can create a deal, which means the vast majority are relegated to supporting roles.

Is Hollywood racist per se? On the one hand, there is too much money to lose by categorically excluding a substantial segment of the population, particularly one with a lot of consumer power. On the other, there's no denying that Hollywood is very much an old boy's network in which who you know counts more than what you know. As such, the structure has effectively excluded many blacks from participation.

People like to believe that an actor or actress with enough talent will succeed. If these performers are black and they don't make it, then the blame falls to racism. But the idea that talent conquers all in Hollywood is yet another myth. Rarely does an actor become a superstar unless he or she has the right agent and the right assistance. If a performer does not have friends in positions of power, he or she will not get work. It has little to do with talent or ability. This reality has left a lot of people outside the loop, not just black performers and filmmakers. Few women ever become directors or producers, for example. (Debbie Allen remains a rarity—and she's yet to get a directing job outside of television.)

Theater owners also play a big role in making or breaking a film. A movie's success generally is based on the number of screens that will show it, and owners like to hedge their bets by supporting sequels and the moneymaking superstars who can draw large crowds. A blockbuster film requires two thousand screens, while a moderately successful hit, with roughly $100 million in receipts requires fifteen hundred screens. With less than a thousand screens committed to show a movie, the backers are taking a big chance.

The number of screens needed to make money also depends on the movie's cost, of course. Many of Woody Allen's films, for example, are financially successful even though they fall short of being box-office hits. Allen's movies show primarily in urban areas such as New York, Los Angeles, and San Francisco because theater owners in the Midwest and South know that his brand of comedy may not appeal to their audiences. Allen is successful, in part, because he recognizes these factors and shoots his films on a relatively modest

Cleopatra Jones (1973): Tamara Dobson

Trick Baby (1973): Mel Stewart with Kiel Martin

Willie Dynamite (1973): Joyce Walker and Roscoe Orman

budget, bringing them in on schedule after writing, directing, and often starring in his productions.

In the end, few contemporary performers will reach the point that their names alone draw a huge audience. Those who do, however, have tremendous potential to change the status quo in Hollywood. An Eddie Murphy could single-handedly improve the situation for other blacks in various ways. He could insist, for example, that a certain number of positions on his movies be filled by talented blacks. He could set aside a percentage of his salary to help put writers, directors, and other artists to work. And he could persuade the studios to support special projects that have meaning for the American black. Much like a Steven Spielberg, an artist as popular as Murphy has a lot of clout with studios. Even if the project may not make money, the studios generally have no choice but to go along with it.

Some black performers, notably Sidney Poitier, Bill Cosby, and one or two others have used their

Three Tough Guys (1973): Isaac Hayes

power to effect change. Each has done much to support the black artist by ensuring that black actors and staffers work on his productions. Murphy, on the other hand, makes a lot of money but we don't know how much he does to assist others. He has yet to make a statement with his work. After seeing a Murphy film, one is left with the uneasy feeling that he doesn't care at all for the audience. I get the feeling he is a part of the "Black Pack" that acts solely for itself and, much like the Brat Pack, treats everything as a sort of inside joke.

The new independent filmmakers, such as Spike Lee and John Singleton, may be able to accomplish what Murphy has not by serving as a catalyst for black performers, writers, and technicians. Undoubtedly, the success of Lee's films has been responsible in part for the wave of black-experience films of the early 1990s. Not only were these movies honest and realistic in the images they project, but they also gave more blacks a chance to show their talent. According to a *New York Times Magazine* article, the crew of Singleton's first film, *Boyz N the Hood*, was ninety percent black, a remarkable accomplishment in and of itself.[13]

---

[13]Bates, Karen Grigsby, "They Gotta Have Us," *New York Times Magazine*, July 14, 1991, p. 15.

I Escaped From Devil's Island (1973): Jim Brown with Paul Richards

Slaughter's Big Rip-Off (1973): Jim Brown and Judy Brown

The Slams (1973): Jim Brown

51

That Man Bolt (1973): Fred Williamson

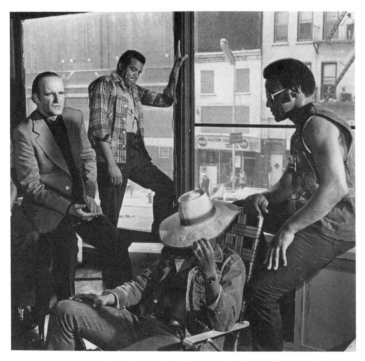

Crazy Joe (1973): Fred Williamson (right) with Peter Boyle (left)

Truck Turner (1974): Yaphet Kotto

The Spook Who Sat by the Door (1973): Larry Cook and Janet League

Black Caesar (1973): Fred Williamson (with cigar) surrounded by Don Pedro Colley, Julius Harris, and Phillip Roye

Sheba, Baby (1974): Austin Stoker and Pam Grier

54

Thomasine and Bushrod (1974): Vonetta McGee and Max Julien

The Klansman (1974): Lola Falana and O. J. Simpson with Richard Burton

Truck Turner (1974): Annazette Chase and Isaac Hayes

Black Samson (1974): Carol Speed and Rockne Tarkington

The Take (1974): Billy Dee Williams

Hell Up in Harlem (1974): Fred Williamson and Margaret Avery

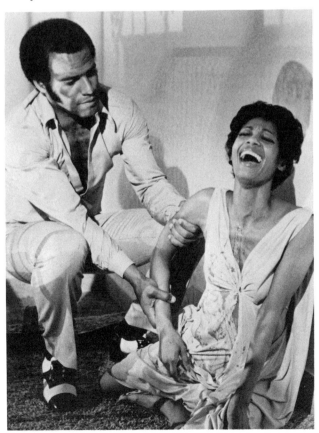

57

Huckleberry Finn (1974): Paul Winfield and Odessa Cleveland

Foxy Brown (1974):
Antonio Fargas, Pam
Grier, and Terry Carter

Claudine (1974):
James Earl Jones and
Diahann Carroll

Cleopatra Jones and the Casino of Gold (1974): Tamara Dobson

Bamboo Gods and Iron Men (1974): James Inglehart and Shirley Washington

Abby (1974): William Marshall

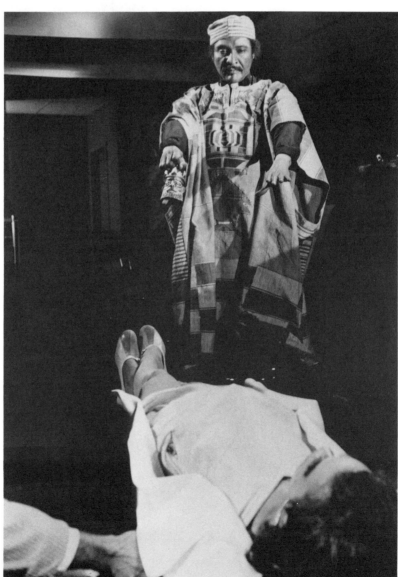

61

Amazing Grace (1974):
Rosalind Cash, Moses
Gunn, and "Moms"
Mabley

The Education of Sonny Carson (1974): Joyce Walker and
Rony Clanton

Black Belt Jones (1974): Jim Kelly and Gloria Hendry

Blazing Saddles (1974): Cleavon Little

Uptown Saturday Night (1974): Sidney Poitier and Rosalind Cash

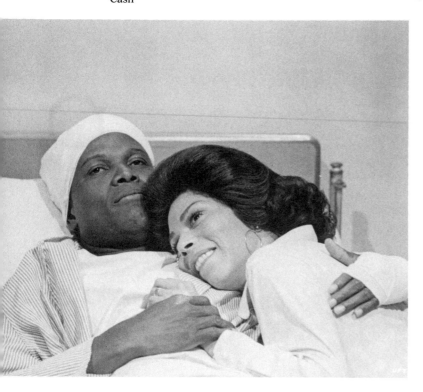

Black Eye (1974): Fred Williamson and Richard Anderson

64

Sugar Hill (1974): Marki Bey

Sidekicks (TV, 1974): Louis Gossett Jr. with Larry Hagman and Jack Elam

Saturday Night Live (TV, 1975): Garrett Morris

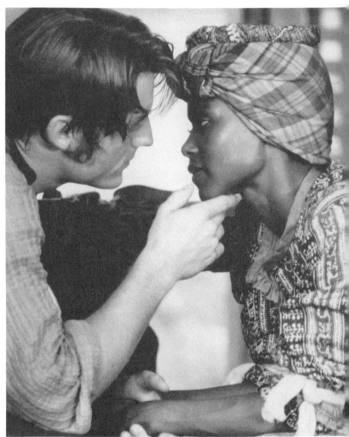

Mandingo (1975): Brenda Sykes with Perry King

Mandingo (1975): Ken Norton with Perry King

Lady Cocoa (1975):
Lola Falana

Diamonds (1975):
Richard Roundtree with
Robert Shaw

Man Friday (1975): Richard Roundtree with Peter O'Toole

Friday Foster (1975): Yaphet Kotto and Carl Weathers

Report to the Commissioner (1975): Yaphet Kotto with Michael Moriarty (right)

Cooley High (1975): Glynn Turman (seated) and
Lawrence-Hilton Jacobs

Mahogany (1975):
Billy Dee Williams

A Piece of the Action (1977): Sidney Poitier and Bill Cosby

4

Superstars: Transcending or Perpetuating Stereotypes?

In today's superstar environment, the performers who reach the top can have an enormous impact. By choosing their projects and characters conscientiously, famous actors and actresses can serve as inspiring role models for others. Achieving a strong box office appeal, these stars can exert a lot of influence with producers and studio heads. But how have various black superstars put their power and influence to use? Not surprisingly, some have done much to serve as positive role models, while others have made either negative statements through their choice of characters and material or no statement at all.

The Megabuck Stars of the Late Seventies and Eighties

Many people look upon the 1980s as the quintessential decade of selfishness and greed. The eighties gave us the "Me Generation," the yuppie phenomenon, and Ronald Reagan's Hollywood presidency. Perhaps nothing portrayed the rise

and fall of avarice so well as Wall Street's notorious junk bond. All in all, they marked the decade of high profits and, many would argue, little substance.

It's fitting, then, that the eighties also stamped the golden age of Hollywood hype. While studios and agents have always promoted profitable actors, the 1980s saw the rise of an entirely new breed of superstar. Nothing was too big for a decade of such expansion, it seems, and Hollywood capitalized on this pervasive attitude by creating megabuck stars. Artists evoking even a hint of popular appeal were packaged, promoted, and foisted upon the public in record numbers.

The print and television media responded by running a perpetual contest of sorts. Headlines such as "The Sexiest Man Alive," "The New Marilyn," "The Funniest . . ." and "The Best . . ." bombarded us from every corner, creating an enormous amount of publicity for stars. Cybill Shepherd and Bruce Willis, for example, both arose from the banal origins of the television show *Moonlighting*.

Leadbelly (1975): Roger E. Moseley

Mahogany (1975): Diana Ross

Cornbread, Earl and Me (1975): Keith Wilkes and Bernie Casey

Hustle (1975): Paul Winfield with Ben Johnson and Burt Reynolds

Boss Nigger (1975): Fred Williamson

Cornbread, Earl and Me (1975): Larry Fishburne III and Rosalind Cash

And each, at various times, has been billed as "The Most Eligible," "The Sexiest," and just about any other glitzy superlative one can imagine.

Some might argue the degree of their talent but not on their glamour, stars such as Willis and Shepherd made rapid ascents and lots of money. In the process, however, they have had little impact on Hollywood or on society at large. As with the junk bond, the hype was there with many of these superstars but the substance never quite materialized. Twenty years from now, how many of us will be impressed by Hollywood's claim to have found "The Next Cybill Shepherd" or "The Hottest New Actress Since Kathleen Turner"?

Black performers also joined the race for fame and fortune, gaining tremendous popularity in all areas of entertainment. Michael Jackson became one of the decade's most popular and successful rock stars, Oprah Winfrey became the queen of the television talk shows, and Bill Cosby rose to the top of the Nielsen rating. Whoopi Goldberg, Eddie Murphy, and Richard Pryor became leading comedians. While all achieved superstar status, the amount of substance behind the public image has differed.

In some cases, the fame was supported by real talent and a contribution to others. Cosby, for one, has dedicated himself to offering positive role models and creating opportunities for black artists in the field of television. His show has been

Adios Amigo (1975): Fred Williamson

Take a Hard Ride (1975): Jim Brown and Fred Williamson

criticized as little more than a black *Father Knows Best*. But whether or not this is a useful criticism, few people can question Cosby's commitment and sincerity. He has opened the door to many young black artists and provided American audiences across the nation with a new perspective on black middle-class families. The success of the show has been a landmark in television history.

It is more difficult, however, to evaluate the substance and contribution of other black performers. Oprah Winfrey, for example, can be a brilliant actress in dramatic roles (e.g. *The Color Purple* on the big screen; *The Women of Brewster Place* on the small) and her daytime talk show often covers controversial and thought-provoking issues and has made her the most powerful black woman in the field of entertainment. During these shows, she appears to be truly concerned about the issues. But at other times, Winfrey's show comes across as tacky and downright embarrass-

ing. One example was a show about "white collar women and blue collar men." A group of men were lined up so that women from the audience could choose three, ask each a question and then make their choice. The women chose the men with designations such as, "I'll take Plaid Shirt and Leather Jacket in the second row, and Blond Hair in the first row." The process was then reversed so the men who were not yet chosen could line up three women from the audience. Winfrey herself admitted that this was not one of her more socially conscious programs.

Other black performers have achieved huge stardom and made a tremendous amount of money, yet offered very little in return. Eddie Murphy and Richard Pryor stand out in this category. Apart from being black comedians, these two personalities have a lot in common. Both use profanity and sexual innuendo freely in their performances, speak in a fast-paced, "badass" style of jive and use both their race and comic license to slur the "uncoolness" of being white. Both are successful "crossover" artists who draw their popularity from white and black audiences alike. While few would question the ability of these two men to entertain and amuse, there is considerable room for debate on the import of their contributions to American film history.

In the mid-1980s, Pryor became so popular that Hollywood, purportedly, gave him $50 million to develop and star in a series of movies. The result was a string of box-office flops, typified by the autobiographical *JoJo Dancer*. A colossal failure on every level, it was puerile, poorly acted and chock-full of clichés and profanity. The all-too-obvious intent was to justify Pryor's personal use of crack. His Mama was a whore, his Daddy didn't understand him, and even his wife refused to support him when he gave up his job as a hog-gutter and set out to become a comedian.

Rather than evoking sympathy, Pryor's self-centered, scatologically-tinged performance leaves one sorely disappointed, not only in the movie itself but in the wasted opportunity. Here is a black actor who had the opportunity and the finances to make any statement he wanted. He could have

Bucktown (1975): Thalmus Rasulala and Fred Williamson

77

Aaron Loves Angela (1975): Moses Gunn

hired the best scriptwriters, created meaningful roles for other blacks, and done something to rectify the social injustices against which he rails. Instead, he chose to promote only himself and even failed at that.

While Eddie Murphy's film career has eclipsed that of Pryor, we could ask, what had he done to uplift his audience. Granted, his films are frequently funny and entertaining; some scenes will be remembered for years to come. The bath scene in *Coming to America*, for instance, shows a maiden surfacing from Eddie's bath to announce, "The royal penis has been washed." As Alex Foley, the *Beverly Hills Cop* character, Murphy is witty, charming, and hilariously profane as he creates mayhem and chaos with his fast-talking jive. In a scene at the Beverly Hills Palm, Foley's uproar about bigotry gets him into the room he wants; later, he shatters the poise of a voluptuous (white) secretary when he feigns the delivery of highly explosive materials. In reality, the brown paper bag he carries contains vitamin pills.

Undeniably, Murphy is a great entertainer. But with all the clout he has gained as a major star, the question remains, "Is that all there is?" As Murphy soared to superstardom, the formulae for his movies became increasingly centered around Murphy at the expense of his fellow actors. In his earlier films, Murphy played costar roles with the likes of Nick Nolte in *48 HRS* and Dan Aykroyd in *Trading Places*. His roles, the well-written scripts, and skilled direction all came together to make Murphy shine. Whether the other players effectively carried Murphy or masked a deficit of acting ability is a matter of opinion. But few can deny that by the time Murphy made movies such as *Golden Child* and *Harlem Nights*, much of the spell had been broken.

Aaron Loves Angela (1975): Kevin Hooks and Irene Cara

Old Dracula (1975): Teresa Graves with David Niven

Golden Child opens in a Tibetan monastery as a child prodigy of mystical abilities is crowned to a position of high rank. The movie cuts to New York City, where we learn that the child, whose mission is to save the world, has been kidnapped. The usual clutter of action, adventure, and loud music accompany Murphy as he—you guessed it—finds the child and saves the world. Besides being sophomoric and predictable, the movie is a poor imitation of fantasy/adventure films such as *Raiders of the Lost Ark*. While *Golden Child* makes an amusing home video rental, it scarcely rates as quality entertainment. A few more like this and Murphy

seemed indeed on his way to becoming the Burt Reynolds of the 1990s.

Perhaps Murphy, like other performers who have become famous extremely quickly, did not have time to mature as an artist. When a star reaches his level of popularity, few will dare to question him—why argue with success? While this may be a comfortable position for Murphy, his films of the late 1980s certainly suggest that he could have accepted some constructive criticism. In his live concert film *Raw*, for instance, was it really necessary for Murphy to describe his bowel movement? In graphic detail? For five minutes? Is bathroom humor required at this stage of his career?

Murphy's fast talk succeeded in getting him noticed and even bringing him fame. But the American public tires rapidly of "shtick," and Murphy himself needs to evolve and develop as an artist. In *Coming to America* and most of his later endeavors, Murphy's endless stream of "f--- you's" not only are hostile and offensive but also suggest an ignorance of the English language. That ignorance is equaled only by his sexist slurs and belligerent view of women (as sluts, prostitutes, or mindless drones) and many others around him.

Had a white person written or directed *Raw*, an outcry across America would have deemed the film racist and sexist, not to mention pointless. And that raises a number of important questions. Should there be a different standard for black performers than for white? Is the goal of excellence to be thrown aside and forgotten simply because an actor is black? I, for one, believe not. Black performers have shown throughout history that they are just as capable, if not more so, than performers of any other race or color

A Comparison With the Past

Comparisons of people are never entirely fair, given the inherent differences in the individuals and the nature of the times in which they live.

The Wilby Conspiracy (1975): Sidney Poitier with Persis Khambatta

81

Let's Do It Again (1975): Sidney Poitier and Bill Cosby

Analogies can still serve a useful purpose, however, in bringing certain characteristics to light. Compare, for example, Richard Pryor and Eddie Murphy with Paul Robeson and Sidney Poitier. Paul Robeson never achieved the "superstar" status of Murphy or Pryor, largely because the idea of a mainstream black star was still a distant dream in the 1930s and 1940s. But Robeson remains one of the most outstanding actors in American film history, despite the lack of public accolades and million-dollar salaries.

His *Emperor Jones* left much to be desired in terms of content and production values, but Robeson himself broke new ground. "Back in 1933, the significance of the film was the presence of Paul Robeson. He was the first strong black image on the screen," says film historian Charles Woods. Robeson's presence, regardless of the role he played, was invariably magnetic. Huge in stature, he represented raw power. Yet his enormous eyes and deep baritone voice emanated sensitivity and a richness of character. Robeson's particular genius lay in his ability to take a poor or limited role and bring it to life.

Unfortunately, racism in America and the political climate of his times deprived Robeson of any real chance to develop his talent here. But he did go on to make more successful films in Europe. *Proud Valley*, for example, was set in a Welsh mining community. To an American viewer, the manner in which the film's whites treat Robeson's character is striking indeed. In the opening scenes,

Let's Do It Again (1975): Jimmie Walker

Let's Do It Again (1975): Lee Chamberlain and Denise Nicholas (blond wig)

Robeson hops into the freight car of a moving train and almost lands on another traveler. The two strike up a conversation and decide to travel together for awhile—that fact that one is black and the other is white does not even enter the picture.

Later, a mine worker who leads the town choir befriends Robeson, taken by his rich voice and personality, and eventually, Robeson moves in with the miner and his family. The film is remarkable not only for its absence of racial tension but also for the role Robeson plays. In *Proud Valley*, he does not portray the young buck or any other Hollywood stereotype, but simply a young man, quiet and dignified, who lives and works much like everyone else in the film.

In comparing Robeson to Murphy and Pryor, the description "understated" comes to mind. As a product of his times, Robeson faced greater racism and less opportunity than most black people today. Yet few talents today possess the brilliance it took to transcend the limited and stereotypical roles that were available to Robeson. For all of his talent, Robeson could expect trivial wages and little public recognition.

Still, when not on the screen, Robeson was a Renaissance man: author, composer, intellectual, and social activist. He genuinely cared about people and was concerned about making the world a better place. This sense of humanity, coupled with a relatively lesser concern for himself, may have

The Shark's Treasure (1976): Yaphet Kotto

Mother, Juggs & Speed (1976): Bill Cosby and friends

been the very ingredient that infused Robeson's stage presence with such vitality. And the lack of it, conversely, may be what leaves one feeling so empty after watching some of Murphy's latest films.

Much like Robeson, Sidney Poitier and Harry Belafonte will be remembered for their extraordi-

nary presences. Almost invariably, their charisma and humanity combined to create unusually rich characters with whom all audiences—black and white alike—could identify. By contrast, Murphy and Pryor often appear to be acting *at* the audience, not with or for them.

Poitier, along with Belafonte, was one of the

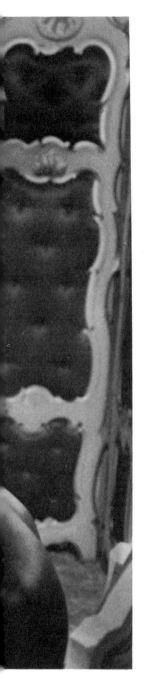

first crossover leading men, a distinction that has brought them a fair amount of criticism from some members of the black intelligentsia. They argue that Poitier made it too easy for white audiences to accept him—that he was too appealing in his "black saint" roles. By understating his sexuality, he represented no threat to the vulnerable ego of the white male. Likewise, Poitier was almost always well-spoken, poised, and restrained, rarely confronting whites about their

Rocky (1976): Carl Weathers as Apollo Creed with Sylvester Stallone

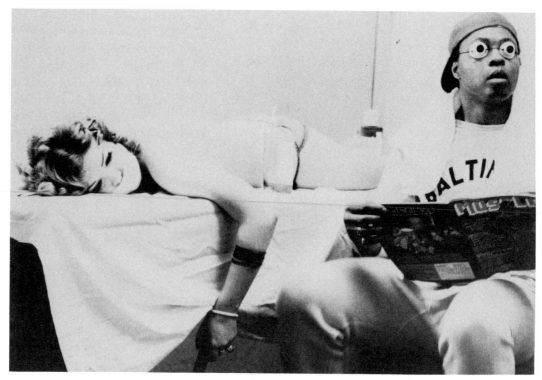

Stay Hungry (1976): Roger E. Moseley

Norman . . . Is That You? (1976): Redd Foxx and Pearl Bailey

racism even in the most provoking of situations. The audience could always count on him to act appropriately and in good taste.

Author Donald Bogle, in his book *Toms, Coons, Mulattoes, Mammies & Bucks*, provides the following analysis of Poitier's popularity: "Poitier's ascension to stardom in the mid-1950s was no accident.... Foremost was the fact that in this integrationist age Poitier was the model integrationist hero. In all his films he was educated and intelligent. He spoke proper English, dressed conservatively, and had the best of table manners. For the mass white audience, Sidney Poitier was a black man who met their standards. His characters were tame; never did they act impulsively, nor were they threats to the system. They were amenable and pliant. And finally they were funky, almost sexless and sterile. In short, they were the perfect dream for white liberals anxious to have a colored man in for lunch or dinner....

"But the second reason for Poitier's ascension was that in many respects his characters were still

Norman . . . Is That You? (1976): Vernee Watson and Michael Warren

Sparkle (1976): Mary Alice, Lonette McKee, and Irene Cara

Pipe Dreams (1976): Gladys Knight

the old type that America had always cherished. They were mild-mannered Toms, throwbacks to the humanized Christian servants of the 1930s. When insulted or badgered, the Poitier character stood back and took it. He knew the white world meant him no real harm. He differed from the old servants only in that he was governed by a code of decency, duty and moral intelligence."[14]

[14]Bogle, Donald, *Toms, Coons, Mulattoes, Mammies & Bucks.* New York: Continuum, 1973, pp. 175–76.

But was Poitier really just another "mild-mannered Tom"? True, his characters did not go around fighting and shooting people every time they were insulted, but that is hardly a sign of weakness or mindless subservience. Poitier always played a strong character who was full of integrity. While the abstention from retaliatory violence may have angered some black activists, Poitier's characters did not simply submit to the injustices of racism.

These very characteristics, in fact, allow Poitier to expose racism quite effectively in *In the Heat of the Night* (1967). Poitier stars as Virgil Tibbs, a black homicide detective from Philadelphia who goes home to visit his mother in the small town of Sparta, Mississippi. At the train station, he is picked up on suspicion of murder, obviously because he is black. The deputy (Warren Oates) tells Tibbs to "Get on your feet, boy" and then takes him to the police station, where he comes face to face with Sheriff Gillespie (Rod Steiger), the quintessential southern bigot.

Hands on his fat belly, smacking gum, Gillespie calls Tibbs "boy" and casts him a suspicious look when he finds money in his wallet. "Where you get that kinda money, boy?" he drawls. "I *work* for it," replies Tibbs forcefully, adding that he makes $162.39 per week, clearly more than Gillespie's southern wages. Throughout the film, Poitier's unflappable calm allows the audience to see the

The Muthers (1976): Jayne Kennedy

truth about racism. Of course his character is angry. Who wouldn't be when confronted with injustice, ignorance, and hatred? But Poitier manages to make his point without the use of vulgarity or violence, thereby offering a valuable role model to us all.

Through his skill as an actor and his compassion as a human being, Poitier transcends the boundaries of race to create a universal character with whom all audiences can relate. Poitier as Virgil Tibbs is hardly an empty stereotype, especially considering that the film was made in the late 1960s. Tibbs holds a responsible job, makes a decent wage, and is an expert in his field. He asks for and commands respect. He is sensitive, intelligent, and dedicated. In one scene, Tibbs is on the telephone with his superior in Philadelphia, who urges him to stay in Sparta and assist with the

Countdown to Kusini
(1976): Greg Morris

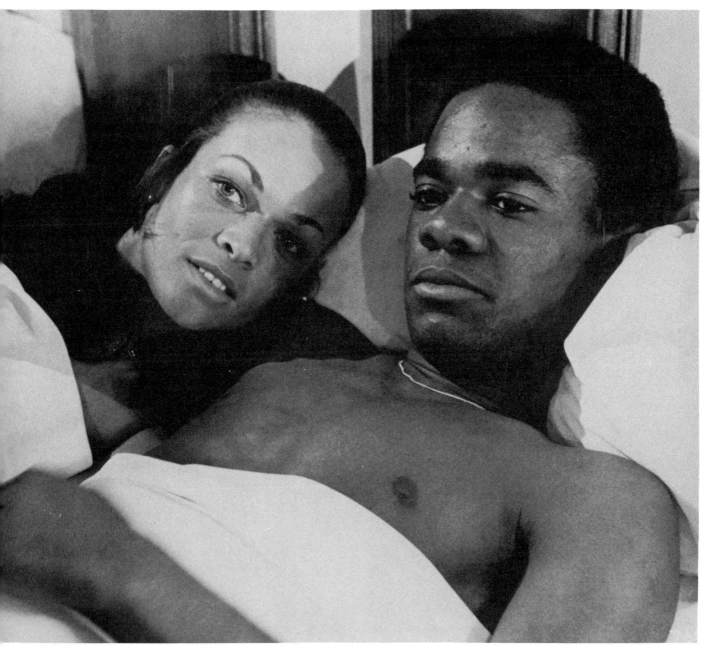

J. D.'s Revenge (1976): Alice Jubert and Glynn Turman

murder case. "Even if I offered help, they wouldn't want it," says Tibbs. "No, sir, no, sir, I'm not prejudiced." Once he decides to stay on, we see a character of incredible fortitude who is committed to doing what he believes is right. We also see Poitier's true pathos come through when Tibbs comforts the (white) wife of the murder victim.

In another scene, Tibbs and Gillespie go to the mansion of Mr. Endicott (Larry Gates), one of the town's leading citizens. When the two find Endicott in his garden, tending orchids, Tibbs impresses him by commenting on a particular variety of orchid. Endicott says that Tibbs's attraction to the flower is appropriate because it, like the Negro, requires special attention to survive. The sparring continues and the tension mounts until Endicott slaps Tibbs across the face. But unlike most of Poitier's characters, who would have chosen to walk away, Tibbs slaps back without a moment's hesitation.

Drum (1976): Ken Norton and Brenda Sykes

Car Wash (1976): Franklin Ajaye (in Afro) and Richard Pryor

The scene had such an impact that it served as a turning point for black characters, says Charles Woods.

During the late sixties, the "Black is Beautiful" movement was taking place. What the growing black urban audiences wanted to see was a black hero who took no stuff from the white man. For more than seventeen years, Poitier had always played the dignified black, the supreme gentleman who was always restrained, despite the racism he had to endure. In *In the Heat of the Night*, Poitier's anger and bitterness reached the boiling point.

97

Dandy, the All American Girl (1976): Franklin Ajaye with Stockard Channing

When the white, racist southerner slapped him and he turned around and slapped that southerner back, that was a slap that was heard around the world. The audience saw this as prophecy. Not only was Poitier striking back as a character in a movie, but he was striking back for all blacks. Not long after that, you had blacks in films being allowed to fight back and win. Before that time, they could get angry but could not fight back. If anyone had to take up the fight for them, it was always their white friend. Black men were not allowed to hit white men back and win.[15]

---

[15] Interview with Charles Woods by Gary Null, March 1, 1990.

Poitier's career also stands out for his choice of characters and films. For many years now, performers have attempted to justify their acceptance of demeaning or moronic roles by saying that it was the only work available and that they needed the money. Robert Townsend made an entire film, *Hollywood Shuffle,* about this dilemma in the mid-eighties. Undeniably, it takes character and forti-tude to turn down a bad role when one needs the money. If one performer turns it down, another is bound to take it. But Poitier has shown that an actor can be successful while not compromising his own integrity or that of his race.

Of course, Poitier's dignity and impeccable manners did contribute to his acceptance, but they did not dilute the impact of his message. Given the

Drum (1976): Pam Grier and Ken Norton

times in which he was functioning, it's almost ridiculous to imagine Poitier being anything other than what he was. And few of today's superstars could have filled his roles. Can you imagine, for example, Eddie Murphy, with his jive-ass, "moth-erf---er" repertoire, chained to Tony Curtis in *The Defiant Ones*? Or what about Richard Pryor cast against the bigoted sheriff played by Steiger in *In the Heat of the Night*?

Sure, Murphy and Pryor are comedians, while Poitier is a dramatic actor. But that does not account for the implausibility of these scenarios. Rather, it is because both Pryor and Murphy have yet to display any real depth of character or sensi-

The Bingo Long Traveling All-Stars & Motor Kings (1976): James Earl Jones and Billy Dee Williams

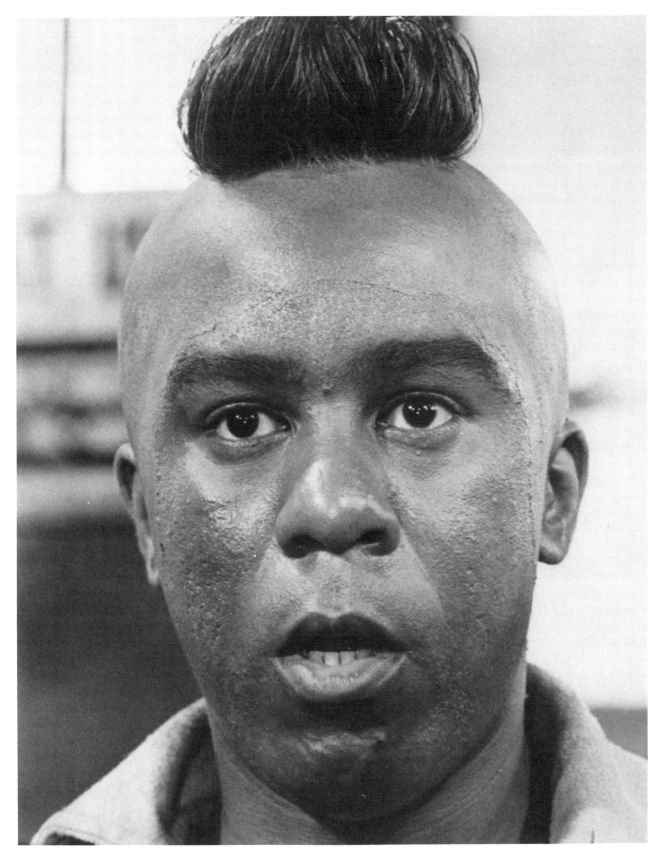

The Bingo Long Traveling All-Stars & Motor Kings (1976): Richard Pryor

tivity. They resort to the facile and often the cheap, going for the lowest common denominator in their comedy. They could possibly learn something from watching Morgan Freeman, James Earl Jones, Danny Glover, and other dramatic actors.

This does not detract from the contributions Murphy and Pryor have in fact made. Their crossover appeal has been unprecedented, sending a message to Hollywood magnates that black talent is indeed a force to be reckoned with. As role models, they have shown black America the road to wealth and fame. Their phenomenal success has paved the way for the next generation of black artists. Gone are the days when black performers will be dismissed out of hand; Hollywood has too much to lose, especially if the one they dismiss turns out to be the next Eddie Murphy.

Silver Streak (1976): Scatman Crothers and Richard Pryor with Gene Wilder and Jill Clayburgh

Death Journey (1976): Fred
Williamson

A Piece of the Action (1977): Denise Nicholas and Hope
Clarke

Young Cassius Clay (1977): Chip McAllister

The Greatest (1977): Muhammad Ali surrounded by Ernest
Borgnine (as Angelo Dundee) and John Marley

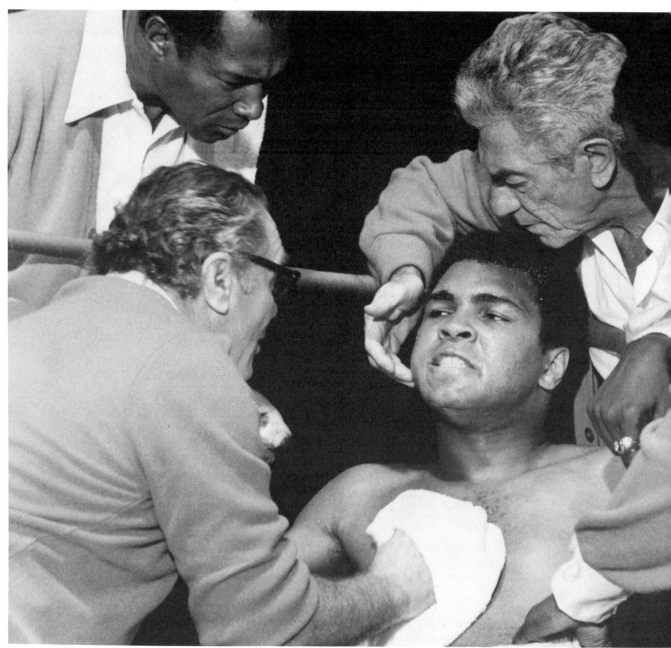

Which Way Is Up? (1977): Lonette McKee and Richard Pryor

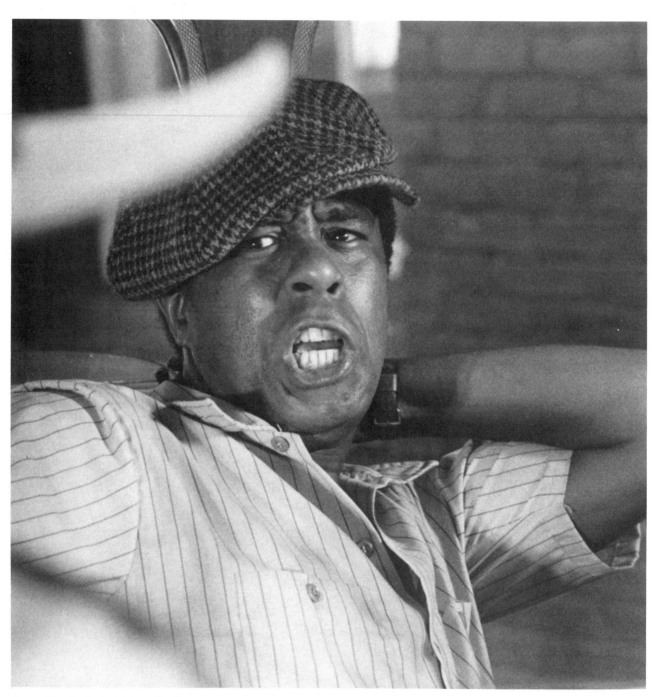

Greased Lightning (1977): Richard Pryor

A Hero Ain't Nothing But a Sandwich (1977): Larry B. Scott, Cicely Tyson, and Paul Winfield

Damnation Alley (1977): Paul Winfield

110

Brothers (1977): Vonetta McGee and Bernie Casey (in poster)

Soap (TV, 1977): Robert Guillaume with Robert Mandan

Good Times (TV, 1977): Jimmie "Dy-no-mite" Walker and Janet Jackson

The Bill Cosby Show (TV, 1978): Cosby surrounded by his television family (clockwise from left) Phylicia Rashad, Sabrina LaBoeuf, Malcolm Jamal Warner, Tempestt Bledsoe, Lisa Bonet, and Keisha Knight Pulliam

Rabbit Test (1978): Jimmie Walker

Fingers (1978): Jim Brown with Tisa Farrow and Harvey
Keitel

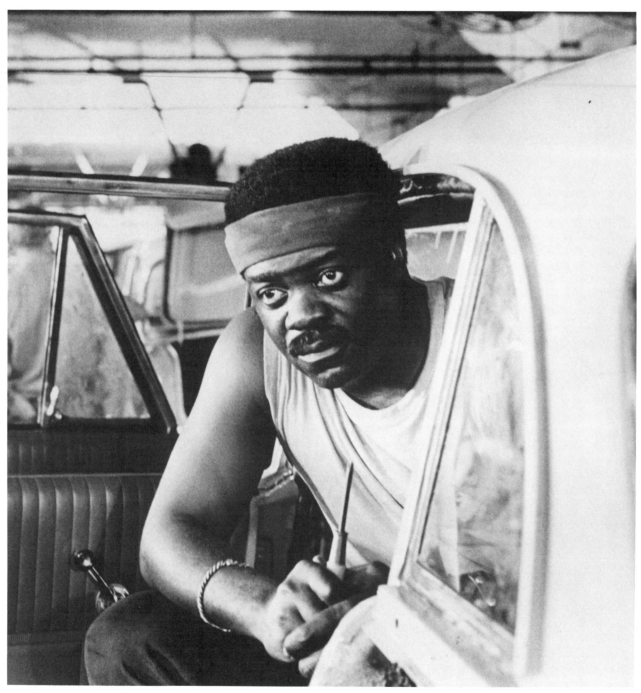

Blue Collar (1978): Yaphet Kotto

The Cheap Detective (1978): Scatman Crothers

Uncle Joe Shannon (1978): Jason Bernard and Madge Sinclair

The Wiz (1978): Ted Ross, Michael Jackson, Diana Ross, and Nipsey Russell

118

California Suite (1978): Gloria Gifford, Richard Pryor, Bill Cosby, and Sheila Frazier

The Glove (1979): Rosey
Grier

119

Roots: The Next Generations (TV, 1979): Dorian Harewood

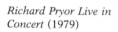

*Richard Pryor Live in
Concert* (1979)

120

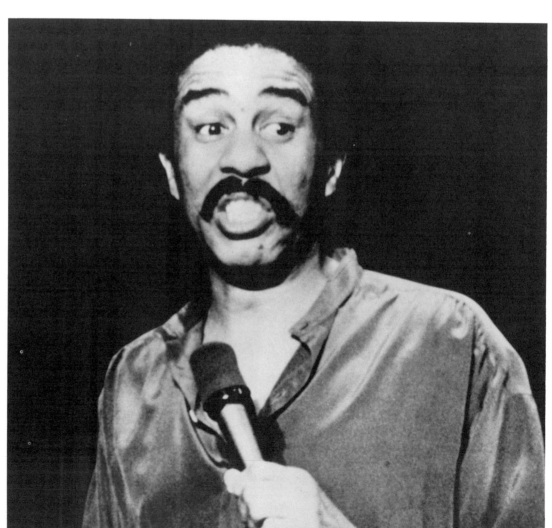

Escape to Athena (1979): Richard Roundtree with Elliott Gould

Apocalypse Now (1979): Albert Hall

Apocalypse Now (1979): Larry Fishburne

Bronco Billy (1980): Scatman Crothers

In God We Trust (1980):
Richard Pryor

122

History of the World—Part I (1980): Gregory Hines

Fame (1980): Irene Cara

Brubaker (1980):
Yaphet Kotto with
Robert Redford and
Matt Clark

The Blues Brothers
(1980): James Brown

Body and Soul (1981):
Leon Isaac Kennedy,
Muhammad Ali, and
Jayne Kennedy on the
set

Stir Crazy (1981): Richard Pryor with Gene Wilder

Bustin' Loose (1981): Cicely Tyson and Richard Pryor

White Dog (1981): Paul Winfield

Nighthawks (1981): Billy Dee Williams

The Sophisticated Gents (TV, 1981): (From left, seated) Roosevelt Grier, Paul
Winfield, and Melvin Van Peebles; (standing) Ron O'Neal, Thalmus Rasulala,
Bernie Casey, Dick Anthony Williams, Raymond St. Jacques, and Robert Hooks

Ragtime (1981): Howard E. Rollins

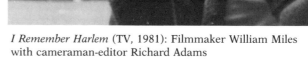

I Remember Harlem (TV, 1981): Filmmaker William Miles with cameraman-editor Richard Adams

Ragtime (1981): Debbie Allen

A Letter From Booker T. (TV, 1981): Ruby Dee and Ossie Davis

48 HRS. (1982): Eddie Murphy with Nick Nolte

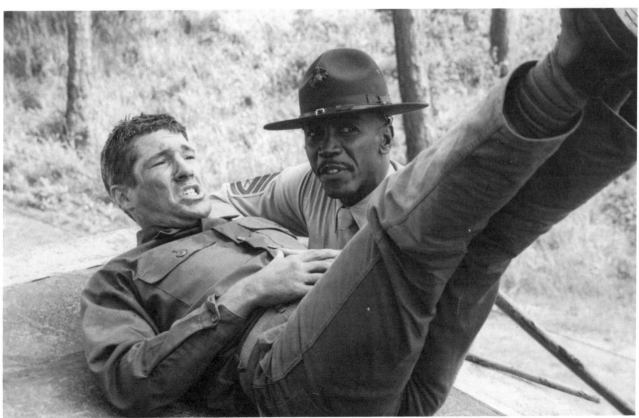

An Officer and a Gentleman (1982): Louis Gossett Jr. with Richard Gere

Rocky III (1982): Carl Weathers

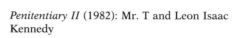
Penitentiary II (1982): Mr. T and Leon Isaac Kennedy

Rocky III (1982): Mr. T with Sylvester Stallone

Cocaine and Blue Eyes (TV, 1982): O. J. Simpson

One Down, Two to Go
(1982): Jim Brown and
Fred Williamson

Star Trek II: The Wrath of Khan (1982): Paul
Winfield

Conan the Barbarian (1982): James Earl Jones with Valerie
Quennessen

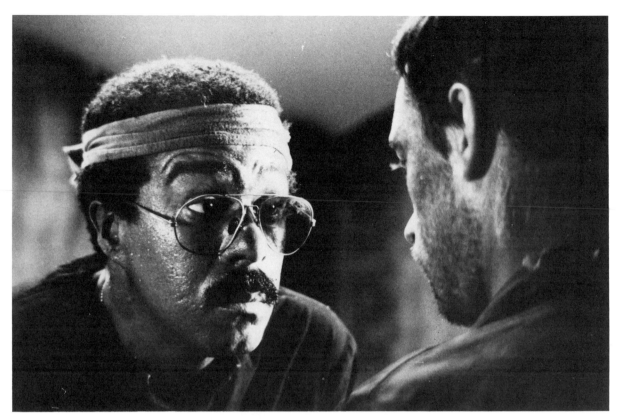

Some Kind of a Hero (1982): Richard Pryor with Ray Sharkey

Richard Pryor Live on the Sunset Strip (1982)

Spike Lee's *Joe's Bed-Stuy Barbershop: We Cut Heads* (1982)

The Toy (1982): Richard Pryor with Ned Beatty (left) and Don Hood

Bill Cosby, Himself (1983)

135

Women of San Quentin (TV, 1983): Yaphet Kotto with Amy Steel

Richard Pryor Here and Now (1983)

For Love and Honor (TV, 1983): Yaphet Kotto with Gary Grubbs (standing), Cliff Potts, and Shelley Smith

Return of the Jedi (1983): Billy Dee Williams with Chumbuka, Harrison Ford, and Carrie Fisher

Trading Places (1983): Eddie Murphy with Dan
Aykroyd

Emmanuelle 4 (1983): Deborah Power (right) with Mia
Nygren as Emmanuelle

The Last Flight (1983): Fred Williamson

137

Superman III (1983):
Richard Pryor with
Christopher Reeve

The Cotton Club (1984): Gregory
Hines and Lonette McKee

The Jesse Owens Story (TV, 1984): Dorian Harewood

The Cotton Club (1984): Maurice and Gregory Hines

Master Harold . . . and the Boys (TV, 1984): Zakes Mokae
with Matthew Broderick

Places in the Heart (1984): Danny Glover

The Vegas Strip Wars (TV, 1984): James Earl Jones

A View to a Kill (1984): Grace Jones

Purple Rain (1984): Apollonia Kotero and Prince

Beverly Hills Cop (1984):
Eddie Murphy

Best Defense (1984):
Eddie Murphy

142

The Brother From Another Planet (1984): Joe Morton

Mad Max Beyond Thunderdome (1985): Tina Turner

Go Tell It on the Mountain (TV, 1984): Olivia Cole and Paul Winfield

Miami Vice (TV, 1984): Philip Michael Thomas with Don Johnson

Iron Eagle (1985): Louis Gossett Jr.

144

Once Bitten (1985):
Cleavon Little

Certain Fury (1985): Irene Cara with Tatum O'Neal

Jo Jo Dancer, Your Life Is Calling (1985): Richard Pryor

145

Brewster's Millions (1985): Richard Pryor with John Candy

Crossroads (1985): Joe Seneca with Ralph Macchio

Badge of the Assassin (TV, 1985): Yaphet Kotto with James Woods

The Last Dragon (1985): Taimak and Julius J. Carry III

White Nights (1985): Gregory Hines with
Mikhail Baryshnikov

147

White Nights (1985):
Gregory Hines with
Isabella Rossellini

Ratboy (1986): Robert Townsend and John Witherspoon with
Christopher Hewitt

Firewalker (1986): Louis Gossett Jr. with Chuck Norris

Captain Eo (1986): Michael Jackson

Soul Man (1986): James Earl Jones

Under the Cherry Moon (1986): Prince

Running Scared (1986): Gregory Hines

Glory (1989): Denzel Washington

5
A Look at Quality

We all know when we have seen a wonderful movie because something inside of us has been touched. We leave the theater with a sense of enrichment, feeling good about life. But despite these intangible responses, the qualities that make a film great are not always easy to pinpoint and describe. Indeed, no one can be certain that a film will be great until it is put together. Even the best script and most talented performers may fail to produce an exceptional movie for reasons that remain something of a mystery. A set formula for excellence simply does not exist.

Generally, the best movies focus either on the more uplifting aspects of life or on the struggle of the human spirit against some negative circumstance rather than draw upon explicit profanity, violence, or sexuality. Individuality also comprises one of the major elements of excellence. On the following pages, we will take a look at some of the better films of the 1950s through 1980s, exploring the factors that make them high-quality productions and set them apart from the average movie.

Glory:

Following the deluge of cliché and routine films that paraded across American screens in the seventies and eighties, *Glory* came as a breath of fresh air. Released in late 1989, it chronicles the history of the Massachusetts 54th Regiment, the first all-black fighting unit raised from volunteer recruits in the North. *Glory* does not use the American Civil War as a mere backdrop for a familiar Hollywood genre, such as the romance in *Gone With the Wind*. Instead, the magnitude of the historical events are allowed to speak for themselves. And speak they do. In portraying the formation and evolution of the 54th Regiment, *Glory* tells a tale that effectively rewrites history and adds a richness to the cultural heritage of all Americans.

Historically, *Glory* marked a cinematic milestone by setting the record straight. Most Americans know little of the important role blacks have played in nearly all of our nation's armed struggles (at least until Vietnam). The film also shows the types of obstacles black men faced when they chose to enlist in the Union Army. They were threatened with automatic enslavement if captured alive by Confederate troops. And the racism coming from the self-proclaimed "abolitionists" of the North, the brothers-in-arms of the 54th Regiment, was equally obvious and abhorrent. The black troops were paid lower wages, denied uniforms and even shoes, and assigned work in the labor battalions because they were not trusted on the front lines.

Glory delivers a sensitive treatment of these issues. While the film focuses on the heroism and integrity of the black troops, the audience's involvement derives from masterful portrayals of the individual characters. The usual empty stereotypes are cast aside as the movie develops people with real emotions and real reactions to the world around them. As the hints of racism are dropped, one can feel the emotions so skillfully enacted by Denzel Washington in his Academy Award-winning role of Trip, a runaway slave. And the restraint of Rawlins, played by Morgan Freeman, shows a power of spirit that is indeed inspiring. Throughout the film, the heroism of the 54th Regiment comes as much from the depth and richness of its members as from its military capabilities.

The film does a remarkable job of developing and balancing its many characters. No one man or event dominates the story; rather, the overriding image is of a group of men working together in the face of turmoil and momentous historical forces. The casting, the character development, and the plot all support this goal. Matthew Broderick, for instance, provides a splendid portrait in his role as Col. Robert Gould Shaw, the mild-mannered, twenty-five-year-old white abolitionist from Boston who undertakes the formation and command of the 54th. Even so, Broderick's acting and his role as the white leader of a black regiment do not eclipse the stature and performances of the others. His character is but one of the many rich and complex roles that work in unison.

Among the black characters, some of the usual "types" exist, but they are far from superficial roles. Both the stature of the actors and the richness of the characters they portray add a dimension to *Glory* that other films often lack. Denzel

Glory (1989): Jihmi Kennedy (left), Denzel Washington, and Morgan Freeman

Washington has described his Trip this way: "The guy I play in *Glory* is raw and rough—a field Negro, not a house Negro, and he's a real survivor. He's wild, rebellious, and very angry. Many of the black soldiers who fought, much like the character I play, went on to become scouts. They were very well-equipped at survival. They were used to living in caves and doing whatever they could to stay out of the reaches of their master.

"Trip is a young man who refused to be broken. He is a product of racism who has become a racist. He basically hates all white people, especially

Morgan Freeman, for his part, turns in one of his best performances as Rawlins, the only black in the regiment to become a sergeant major. Freeman is a unique talent who personally defies all the stereotypes—he is not young, not particularly handsome, and rarely comic. Yet he presents the pure mastery of his character, much as Cicely Tyson does in her performances, and is invariably brilliant.

Freeman has made the following comments on his role in *Glory:* "Rawlins starts off as a gravedigger at Antietam, finds his way to Massachusetts, and in the six to eight months it takes to get into battle, he makes sergeant major. He does not think much beyond the task at hand. He is simply always there, providing inspiration, encouragement, and support to his men. If they start to lose their nerve, his presence speaks, 'Face your enemy.'

"This is not a typical Hollywood theme, and black subjects are not typical Hollywood subjects, but I feel the country is ready to embrace the corrections of history that this film represents. This is the kind of picture that gives legitimacy to the history of people of color and tells us who we are."[17]

Undoubtedly, *Glory* is an important film. Its contents are an illumination of history, not a rewrite of it, and give our black American soldiers the "glory" and respect they deserve. And the film production itself goes beyond the usual standards of Hollywood. Great effort was taken to make the film true to life in its scenes, its characters, and its props. The acting is superb. When leaving the theater, viewers know they have experienced something of true quality.

A Soldier's Story:

This unusual drama, released in 1984, also centers around a troop of black soldiers. The story is set on a Louisiana military base in 1944, a time in which America's fighting troops were still segregated. The racism of the era interlaces the film. It's appalling to think that at a time when the nation had plenty of real enemies to worry about, it also created false ones within the ranks of its own armed forces.

In essence, *A Soldier's Story* is a "whodunit." When an intensely disagreeable black officer, arrogant Sergeant Waters (Adolph Caesar), is shot

Confederates. Eventually he makes a turnaround in his life. I believe he comes to realize this is not where the future of his people lies."

Washington admits that he had reservations about accepting the role. "I've been very hesitant about doing 'slave films,' but the bottom line is that as a black American, that's my history," he said. "I don't know if many people realize that black soldiers in the Union Army were credited with almost turning the tide in the Civil War and giving the advantage to the North."[16]

[16]Press release from TriStar Pictures, 1989.
[17]Ibid.

A Soldier's Story (1984): Howard E. Rollins

156

down in cold blood, an officer from Washington arrives to look into the murder. The officer, Captain Davenport (Howard E. Rollins) sent to investigate is also black, as are all of the other significant characters in the film. The racial tensions established at the outset provide a perfect backdrop for a murder mystery. Fingers are pointed, the killers seem obvious, and only at the end do we find that the least likely of suspects—two young and promising black soldiers—committed the crime.

The mystery genre works to perfection in *A Soldier's Story* (adapted by black dramatist Charles Fuller from his Pulitzer Prize-winning *A Soldier's Play*). The characters and the racism that motivates so many of their actions provide as great a sense of mystery as the plot. And the fast-paced and intriguing story line keeps you guessing until the last, in sharp contrast to many of the formula movies released in the seventies and eighties. Hollywood made many such films because it knows that mysteries, cops and robbers, and action-adventure stories make big money. But the audience often figures out the ending halfway through the movie. Unfortunately, this seems to happen more frequently when the lead stars are black, as in *Lethal Weapon* and *Golden Child*.

A Soldier's Story not only avoids that trap but also manages to develop a full cast of characters into interesting and complex individuals, a feat that few Hollywood movies accomplish. As the Captain conducts individual interviews of the men concerning the murder of Sergeant Waters, we note that each sees events differently. The interviews give us a mirror into their souls and feelings. As each gives his insights on the murder, we also become acquainted with the people he discusses.

Certain stereotypes are present in the film, but only to give them a life of their own. The character C.J., for instance, is a soft-spoken guitar player from the South and the star of the baseball team—easygoing, good tempered, handsome, and a miracle on the field. Everyone loves C.J.—everyone, that is, except Sergeant Waters himself, whose all-consuming loathing of C.J. somehow only grows as the story progresses.

At first, we do not entirely understand what causes Waters's obsessive hatred of C.J.—again, it's a mystery—but hints dropped along the way allow viewers to draw their own conclusions about the inner workings of the sergeant's tormented mind. Finally, just before sending C.J. to the solitary confinement that kills him, Waters explains the insane rage he feels against this young soldier. "Guys like you are homey kinda niggers. Whenever the white man needed someone to abuse, they called on you. We can't have that any more. We can't afford you anymore. Now I have you. One less fool for the race to be ashamed of." (Paraphrased).

A soldier named Peterson (Denzel Washington), on the other hand, is the type that Sergeant Waters likes. Peterson is a headstrong, educated black man from the North. But their relationship is also complex. At one point, Peterson even fights with Waters and they almost kill one another. Yet Waters takes to Peterson "because he fights back." Peterson does not have the same respect for Waters. He loathes him, in fact, for his unreasonable discipline and cruelty. Peterson blames Waters when C.J. hangs himself while in solitary. In the end, we learn that it is Peterson's hatred, not racism, that causes Sergeant Waters's death.

The film does not end with a predictable solution to the murder. Had it closed with Peterson's confession, the complexity and pathos of the movie would not have been so well developed. It would have resembled a regular mystery drama instead—once the murder is solved, it's over. But the real mysteries of the movie—the nature of the characters, the issues of morality and racism—remain for the viewer to ponder long after the film ends. As Peterson makes his confession, a gamut of emotions crosses the Captain's face—anger, frustration, disappointment, sadness, and sympathy. "Who gave you the right to judge?" he asks. "Who are you to decide who is fit to be a Negro and who is not?" (Paraphrased).

A Soldier's Story is rich and thought-provoking, typifying screenwriting at its best. The characters are vibrant and alive. The treatment of racial issues is sensitive and insightful. The true quality of the film lies in its transcendence of race (it was directed, incidentally, by Norman Jewison, who is white). Granted, a film that features both a story about blacks and a virtually all-black cast is an achievement in itself. The actors were great not because they were black, however, but because

A Soldier's Story (1984): Art Evans, Larry Riley, and Adolph Caesar

they were fine performers. And while the film was unusual because it took a standard dramatic genre and adapted it to a black setting, that formula in itself would not have kept the audience's attention riveted to the screen. The script kept us guessing about what would happen next, who these characters were, what they were thinking. All of these factors contributed to the film's success.

Sounder:

This 1972 film version of William Anderson's novel (adapted to the screen by Lonnie Elder III), set in Louisiana during the Depression, tells movingly of a black family that struggles against racism and poverty. In the end, the family survives. Simple? Yes. Unusual? Not particularly. And yet *Sounder* also serves as an example of Hollywood at its best. This movie, too, was directed by a white man, Martin Ritt, which may be the reason it was made.

The real beauty of the film lies in the caliber of the acting. Much like Paul Robeson of an earlier era, Cicely Tyson brings a vibrancy to her character, Rebecca, that was probably absent in the script. The same holds true for Paul Winfield as Nathan, her sharecropper husband, and for Kevin Hooks as David, their son.

The story itself is simple: As the film opens, Nathan and young David are hunting for food in the woods with their dog, "Sounder." Nathan comes back empty-handed and ashamed that he can't feed his family. Later that night, he sneaks out and steals a ham from a neighboring smokehouse belonging to the white folk of the community. He is caught and sentenced to hard labor for a number of years. While Nathan is gone, the rest of the family pulls together and manages to continue

158

the sharecropping, accomplishing the impossible out of sheer will. Nathan eventually returns to the family but he has been terribly crippled, presumably by cruel prison guards.

The plot may appear to be somewhat mawkish and sentimental by today's standards, but one must remember that it was filmed during the height of the civil rights movement. *Sounder* made a point that needed to be made, and it did so quite effectively. With the exception of Sidney Poitier's roles, blacks have rarely been portrayed as real people with feelings and emotions. Even rarer have been stories that showed black people interacting and banding together to overcome obstacles. *Sounder* changed that scenario. We see a strong and united family who love and respect each other, support each other's dreams and aspirations, and are willing to go to any lengths to stay together.

Even the film's title reflects the importance of the family unit. When the white authorities take Nathan away, Sounder runs after his master and is shot. The disappearance of the dog signifies the grief of the family, a grief they must contain because they are black people in a white man's world. Heartbroken, David refuses to believe that Sounder is dead. He watches patiently for the dog to return, and eventually Sounder does come home. The dog's return symbolizes the power of hope and the strength of the family.

Sounder exposes racism as an abomination, but it does so in a thoughtful and sensitive way. This is not an angry film, although there is plenty to feel angry about. The movie puts rage on hold, which makes it all the more effective in its chronicle of everyday life in the rural south of the thirties. The audience experiences the bigotry of the white townsfolk; it feels the injustice of Nathan's sentence. Yet viewers are allowed to put all of these pieces together for themselves.

Simple stories about ordinary people rarely make it onto the screen today. Producers seem to feel that a movie must have a superhero, a glamour of sorts, and million-dollar props just to make a point. *Sounder* has none of these, yet its simplicity makes it all the more significant. Nothing in the movie detracts from the realistic, down-to-earth characters. Whether Hollywood is prepared to acknowledge it or not, it is this glimpse of human-ity that makes *Sounder* one of the excellent films our time.

The Learning Tree:

Unlike *Sounder*, which received wide critical acclaim, *The Learning Tree* (1969) never attracted the attention it deserved. But many film aficionados believe that *The Learning Tree*, director-photographer Gordon Parks's autobiographical story about growing up in the 1920s, was a much better film in terms of content and message. In the view of Charles Woods, the mood of the times accounts for this discrepancy. *The Learning Tree* was never quite successful because its message "was not one wanted by the black audience."

In the late 1960s, says Woods, "black audiences wanted to see a 'bad dude' up there on the screen. Images of blacks 'kicking butt.' There was the 'Black is Beautiful' movement. Black audiences just didn't want to see a young boy and his family trying to live in harmony with the white community. They had enough of it. In *The Learning Tree*, there were images of vicious sheriffs killing black people with impunity, and the black audiences simply did not want to see it."

Outside the context of its time, however, *The Learning Tree* is both profound and significant. According to a *Variety* review at the time, it was "apparently the first film financed by a major company to be directed by a Negro." The story, which at first appears mundane, concerns a brief period in the life of Newt Winger (Kyle Johnson), a middle-class black boy growing up in a small Kansas town. But the movie is far from mundane as Parks portrays elements of humanity that transcend both race and time. The specter of racism appears early in the film, although Parks is careful not to overstate it. He simply demonstrates its existence through a series of vignettes on everyday life.

When Newt and some of his friends go to a nearby orchard to steal apples, the white owner, Jake Kiner (George Mitchell), spies them from the road and gives chase. Though he is a poor match for the healthy young kids, Jake manages to grab one, Marcus Savage (Alex Clarke), who turns on him. Marcus, as we have seen, is the victim of a broken home and a very unhappy life and serves as

l of black hatred of white oppres-
caught and sent to a reformatory,
he town's redneck Sheriff Kirky
ots another innocent black man
incident is tragic, a meaningless
d for which the sheriff shows no

Gordon Parks abstains from passing judgment, which adds to the brilliance of the movie. *The Learning Tree* shows us what Parks himself saw as a child. And yet, a childlike innocence remains. Much like young Newt, the adult Parks refuses to give in to the all-consuming hate. In the late 1960s, this philosophy may very well have been seen as a cop-out, just another simple "Tom" lying down to take the abuse rather than standing up to fight. But the message of the film shows otherwise. Parks does not condone the injustices, he simply has his own ideas about how to overcome them. It's not necessarily the right solution, or the only one available, but the one that makes sense to him.

The film contrasts the behavior of Newt and Marcus. After the shooting, the fat, trashy sheriff offers Newt and the other boys money to dive for the body. "Them niggers are good swimmers," he says. In the next scene, Newt and his mother go to the hospital to visit Jake, the white man. Newt apologizes for his part in the incident and offers to work for Jake as compensation. Marcus, on the other hand, responds viciously. He shows no remorse for what he has done, on the grounds that white folk have always treated blacks unfairly. Newt's mother, who works for the judge who will sentence Marcus, pleads "Go lightly on Marcus," knowing that he is in pain and needs tenderness and compassion most of all. The judge sees Marcus as a bad seed, however, and ships him off to the reformatory.

The film's message comes from Newt's mother as the two walk together one day. Newt tells her that he is afraid of dying, although his feelings clearly go much deeper than that. He wants to know how to get over the fear and live life in a way that makes sense. "It's about loving when you feel like hating," she responds, "like telling the truth when you feel like lying." Newt asks if they will live their entire lives in the same small town. "Well," says his mother. "I hope you won't have to live here all your life. It's not all good place, not all bad

place. Sort of like fruit on a tree. Some good, some bad. No matter if you stay or go, think of it like that all your life. Let it be your learning tree."

From that point on, the film becomes clearer in its intent—to show the good and the bad elements of everyday life. The racism and its effect on Newt and his family are bad, no question about it. But life itself is sometimes good, too. Newt begins seeing Arsella Jefferson, a new girl in town, and they fall in love, a young and innocent love. Touching scenes show the two walking through the traditional waist-high fields of flowers, holding hands, and meeting after school. Together they also experience the racism of the community.

Newt's world is shattered when his friend, Chauncy, also begins to show an interest in Arsella. Chauncy is the judge's playboy son, a wealthy white boy with a fancy car and prestige in the community. Chauncy dazzles Arsella with the car and his wealth, perhaps making her believe that her race does not matter. Arsella becomes pregnant and soon reveals that Chauncy is the father. Though Newt is crushed by the turn of events, he still manages to forgive.

No Way Out:

In his Hollywood debut, *No Way Out* (1950), Sidney Poitier shattered the screen stereotypes that were still entrenched at the time. His performance as Luther Brooks, a young intern in a county hospital, set the course for his acting career and planted the seeds for many of his later characters. Poitier in the film is handsome, educated, and compassionate. When faced (probably not for the first time) with the ugliest of prejudice, he remains cool and opts for reason rather than violence.

As in some of his following films, Poitier as Brooks also has a white benefactor, Dr. Wharton (Stephen McNally), who reassures the inexperienced intern when he feels unsure of himself. Wharton lets Brooks know that he does not think of him as some sort of black charity case. "My interest in you, Brooks, is no different than my interest in any other good doctor," he says. Many critics view this type of white-black relationship as patronizing and even demeaning. It's as if the young doctor needs the approval of his white superior to feel good about himself. And the white superior grants his approval only because it is so easy to do so. After all, Brooks is young, well mannered, and obviously well qualified.

Certainly, some degree of cynicism is justified in evaluating the relationship purely on its racial elements. But it is also a relationship of normal interaction, capturing emotions that have to do with being human, not with being black or white. Most young people starting out on a new career, especially one that includes substantial responsibility, will have self doubts at times. If the same film were made today, perhaps it would be more appropriate for Brooks to have a black superior and receive encouragement from a member of his own race. For its time, however, the relationship is significant. We see two people relating to each other as human beings and rising above the racial tensions.

Early in the film, Brooks is on call when two wounded criminals, low-life brothers, are brought to the hospital for treatment. One is delirious, the other loud-mouthed and foul. "I don't want him," snarls Ray Biddle (Richard Widmark), pointing to Brooks. "I want a white doctor." Biddle's point is obvious but important, especially in light of the times. He is poor white trash, crude, full of hatred, and a vicious hood to boot. The sight of an educated black doctor only fuels his extreme loathing, which becomes one of the primary forces of the film.

Brooks examines the unconscious brother, Johnny, who he concludes is suffering from a brain tumor. He performs a spinal tap, but Johnny dies. Ray, who is handcuffed to the next bed, begins screaming, "That nigger doctor killed Johnny." When Ray is held captive, his own sense of power fades and his hatred for Brooks becomes an obsession, as he manages to instigate the other whites from his slum to create a riot in the black neighborhood. Significantly, the blacks are informed of the plan. They arm themselves and fend off the gang of racists.

Ray, meanwhile, escapes from the hospital's prison ward and hides out in his sister-in-law's house where he lures Brooks and shoots him in the arm. But in the scuffle Ray also tears his wounded leg and falls to the ground, writhing in pain. Johnny's ex-wife (Linda Darnell), who hates Ray and everything he stands for, goads Brooks. "Don't

you think I'd like to put the rest of these bullets through his head? I can't, because I've got to live too. He's sick, he's crazy. But I can't kill a man just because he hates me." He ends up cradling the bad-wounded Ray Biddle in his arms.

Some black critics view this scene with skepticism. Author Donald Bogle wrote: "In a purely Christian way, [Brooks] forgives his opponent. . . . What red-blooded American white audiences in this Eisenhower [sic] age of normalcy could not have liked this self-sacrificing black man? What integrationist-aspiring black audience would not be proud of this model of black respectability? Poitier was clearly a man for all races."[18]

While this type of criticism has its place, it does not reveal the whole story. Is it really so terrible for a black man to portray a character whose sense of empathy transcends race? Were audiences applauding Brooks because he did not kill the white man and thus respected his proper station in life? Or was something much deeper taking place? In many ways, the scene positions Brooks as the classic Hollywood hero. He is not a black or white hero, but simply the quintessential one who opts to do the "right" thing. Certainly Brooks had reason to kill Biddle, who represents the racism that oppressed blacks for decades. But much like other great Hollywood heroes, Brooks throws down the gun and walks away from his opponent with contempt. Biddle lies on the ground, wallowing in self pity. "Cry," Brooks tells him. "You're going to live."

In many ways, these words symbolize Poitier's power on the screen. He does not react violently, but neither does he turn the other cheek. He does not raise his voice, but his eyes can cast a scorn that is much more scathing than words. By showing that one can respond to provocation with resources other than anger, Poitier teaches us a lesson. Blacks aren't the only ones to experience oppression and injustice. But responding with violence, or even by losing one's temper, can result in a loss of power.

Poitier, for his part, seldom loses his power (playing the bad guy in *The Lost Man* was an exception). He controls the screen through his characters and his overwhelming presence. He

[18]Bogle, Donald, *Toms, Coons, Mulattoes, Mammies & Bucks.* New York: Continuum, 1973. p. 179.

fights with his words, his wits, and his dignity. In 1958, for instance, he costarred with Tony Curtis in *The Defiant Ones*, as escaped convicts chained together with manacles. Even at this stage of his career, Poitier creates a character of depth and substance that breaks through the long-established stereotypes. In the end, Poitier always comes out a winner—glorified by Hollywood perhaps, but a winner nonetheless.

Book Adaptations:

American authors provide a wealth of material that has yet to be truly tapped by Hollywood. While bestselling writers with wide-appeal novels have become more popular on the screen—Steven King with his horror stories, Judith Krantz with her steamy tales of love and deceit—their books are custom-made for Hollywood and do little to enrich the American public in their adaptation from paper to celluloid. A few exceptions shown on television encouragingly have broaden the awareness and understanding of the black experience—Alex Haley's *Roots* and Ernest J. Gaines's *The Autobiography of Miss Jane Pittman*, most notably (although it was adapted to film by white writer Tracy Keenan Wynn), together with Gloria Naylor's *Women of Brewster Place*, Lonne Elder III's adaptation of Marcy Hedish's novel, *A Woman Called Moses* (about Harriet Tubman), and Melvin Van Peebles's adaptation of *Sophisticated Gents*, taken from John A. Williams's book, *The Junior Bachelor Society*.

Of the big screen adaptations, those for Alice Walker's *The Color Purple* and Richard Wright's *Native Son* (both of them) stand out. This offered a welcome change from the usual Hollywood fare—and a courageous one, box office-wise—in part because the authors originally wrote them with a different audience in mind.

In adapting a book to the screen, some of the depth of the characters and the nuances of the story are typically lost. A book of five hundred or so pages has much more time to develop its characters than does a two-hour film. For that reason, the books must be taken on as special projects and removed from the budgetary and time limitations that govern ordinary movies. That process has occurred with a number of excellent black films, such as Steven Spielberg's production of *The Color Purple* and primetime television's airing of *Roots* and *Miss Jane Pittman*.

The Color Purple:

This feature film contained the sense of splendor that has come to typify a Spielberg production. Throughout the movie, one constantly senses that *Hollywood* is at work. While the grandness of the production does not particularly enhance the story, neither does it take away from it. In the end, the film works. It is well acted and well scripted. And most important, it brings a novel by Alice Walker, an important literary figure in America, to an audience that otherwise might not be exposed to her work.

The Color Purple (1985) was significant in its treatment of a subject rarely touched upon in American films—the plight of a black woman within her own community. Richly told in a semi-autobiographical fashion, it focuses on Celie (Whoopi Goldberg), whose life has been made miserable by brutish men. Her stepfather (Adolph Caesar) rapes her when she is young and then gives her two children away. Soon thereafter, he marries Celie off to her sister's suitor, assuring the groom, Albert (Danny Glover), that Celie is a good worker. Albert, it turns out, equals her stepfather in tyranny. He is mean, insulting and treats her little better than a dog. Celie's only friend in the story is her sister, Natty (Akosua Busia). Albert originally woos Natty and then banishes her from the house when she battles his rape attempts. The focus then shifts to Celie's suffering under Albert's brutalizing and her longing for Natty.

The Color Purple is wholly about black people. Other than one or two scenes in which the strong-willed Sophia (Oprah Winfrey) confronts the white community, few whites appear in the film at all. One gets the impression that author Alice Walker hardly considers them worth mentioning. The movie also makes the point that regardless of the white characters' true personalities—good or bad, racist or not—the black community has its own realities to deal with and its own problems to solve. This reality is quite separate from any interactions that take place between blacks and whites.

By eliminating white participation in the story, *The Color Purple* gives audiences a unique perspective on the black experience. The film illustrates

The Color Purple (1985): Danny Glover and Whoopi
Goldberg

the problems faced by black women within their
community, rather than the struggle of blacks
against whites. Granted, it presents only one woman's point of view and it is sometimes melodra-
matic in its portrayal of men as villains and cads.
But both the book and the movie brought an
important sociological issue to the fore. They did
much to expose the integrity of black women and,
conversely, the bigotry of black men. One need
only look at the films of Eddie Murphy and Richard Pryor to understand the low regard in which
many black men still hold women.

The Color Purple lacks a cohesive plot in the
traditional sense. Instead, it is a story about people
that weaves its way through the lives and interactions of the characters. By necessity, then, these
characters had to retain on film the richness they
possessed in the novel. Otherwise, there would
have been no story. As a result, the movie provides
a large number of actors and actresses with the

The Color Purple (1985): Margaret Avery

opportunity to develop meaningful characters.

Without Spielberg's participation, a Hollywood studio may never had undertaken the project on its own. By adopting *The Color Purple* and making a success of it, Spielberg sent a message to other filmmakers about the impact they can have on a film's content and its ability to reach a wide audience.

Native Son:

Richard Wright's classic novel, *Native Son*, has been adapted for the screen on two occasions after being staged on Broadway in the early forties by Orson Welles, with Canada Lee in the lead. The first production, made on a minuscule budget and released independently in 1950, starred the author himself as the ill-fated main character, Bigger Thomas. A second version was filmed for television in 1986; it featured a brilliant performance by a talented young actor, Victor Love, as Thomas. The costars included Oprah Winfrey as Thomas's mother; Geraldine Page as the family maid, Peggy; Elizabeth McGovern as Mary, a wealthy young white woman who tries to befriend Bigger Thomas; and Matt Dillon as Jan, Mary's boyfriend.

Richard Wright, no ordinary storyteller, wrote complex narratives that include equally complex characters. In *Native Son,* set in 1930s Chicago, he masterfully intertwined the drama of the story with that created by the race relations he explored. It centers on Bigger Thomas, a sullen young black man in his late teens who lives in a tenement building with his mother. Thomas is a powerful character, full of contradictions and intensity. Early in the film, he appears to be a tough malcontent; in fact, he'd rather rob and steal than work for white folks. As the strongest of his circle of friends, he tries to enlist the others in a burglary that eventually fails. In the meantime, his mother, whom he evidently loves and respects, encourages him to take a job as a chauffeur for a white family. Bigger goes to the family's mansion to apply for the job and is immediately hired.

The position entitles Bigger to a clean room of his own, money in his pocket, and all the food he can eat. One can see Thomas's mind turning as he surveys the wonders of his new surroundings. Part of Wright's writing genius lay in his ability to create such scenes but still leave viewers to draw their own conclusions. Is Bigger suspicious? Is he happy? Does he feel powerful? Impotent? Maybe he thinks this is all too good to be true? Perhaps there is a side to him that spurns the luxury? Maybe there's an even stronger side that wants it, but resents the fact that it is coming from a wealthy white family?

These and other questions quickly pass through one's mind as the film progresses. Depending upon the viewer, both the questions and their answers could vary substantially. A black man might see Thomas's situation in one way, while a black woman or a white viewer interprets it in a completely different manner. In any event, Wright possessed a truly astounding ability to use empty space, a pause or the look in a character's eyes to raise such questions.

Wright's choice of whites supports the movie's message about racism. The characters in the film are not poor white trash, Southern gentry, or the usual bigoted rednecks. They are aristocratic Northern liberals. While these, too, are essentially stereotypes, Wright took care to eliminate the characteristics of hypocrisy that would invalidate their good-willed intentions. Indeed, the good faith of the main characters is the very ingredient that makes Wright's point so powerful. All whites are dangerous, regardless of their intentions, not just the blatant racist and bigot.

Bigger's new employers, the Daltons (Carroll Baker and John McMartin), are presented as cultured gentry with a commitment to improving the condition for blacks. Mrs. Dalton, who is blind, offers Bigger a chance to get an education. She informs him that her husband has done a lot for "colored people" and that the man who had the chauffeur's job before Bigger graduated from both

Native Son (1986): Oprah Winfrey and Victor Love

high school and college while working for them. Bigger stays silent through most of his contact with the Daltons, so again the audience must draw its own conclusions about his reactions and even the Daltons' sincerity. These relationships soon become a backdrop for the central action of the story, a complex web of emotions and interactions that develop between Bigger, the Daltons' daughter, Mary, and her boyfriend, Jan, both of whom are dedicated Communists.

The trouble begins when Mr. Dalton asks Bigger to drive Mary to the university. Once in the car, Mary immediately tries to "befriend" Bigger, assuring him that there is no difference between them. Later, she coerces Bigger into taking her to a Communist Party meeting and makes him promise not to tell her parents. When Mary joins up with Jan, the two of them wage a relentless battle to gain Bigger's friendship. They take him to his favorite eating place, sit with him at the table, join him as he eats, and try to determine why he does not trust them.

The pandering and patronizing creates an almost palpable tension in the film. Bigger smells trouble and wants out, but he is a paid employee—paid to do what the Daltons tell him to do. His increasing anxiety is accentuated by the plot line. As his alarm bells ring louder and louder, the external events in the story become increasingly uncomfortable. At one point, Mary gets so drunk that Bigger has to carry her into the house. The image presents a clear sign of danger—the strong black buck with the unconscious white maiden in his arms.

Bigger tries to put Mary to sleep on the living room sofa, but she falls off with a loud thud. He then carries her up the stairs and manages to get her into bed. As he is about to leave, Mrs. Dalton hears the noise and calls out to Mary. Panicking, Bigger puts a pillow over Mary's face to keep her from crying out and accidentally asphyxiates her.

The gruesomeness of the events that follow reveal Wright's perception of black-white relations. Had Bigger been a white man, these events may never have occurred in the first place. If they had, a white man could have explained that it was a terrible accident, with at least a fifty-fifty chance of proving his innocence. But as a black man, Bigger knows his sentence will be immediate and severe. This sense of finality and hopelessness causes him to stuff Mary's still-warm body into a trunk and drag it to the basement. In a graphic struggle, he slowly feeds her body into the furnace.

Bigger does very little speaking throughout the film, despite his leading role. Even after he goes to prison, he refuses to defend himself. Only in the final scene does Bigger give some indication of the enormous rage he feels. He hates Mary Dalton. She wanted to hear how "Negroes" lived; she made him feel degraded. "White folk live apart," he says. As a black man, he knew he was dead the moment he walked into Mary Dalton's room.

The issue of hopelessness runs throughout the book and movie. In the beginning, Bigger seems to be on the road to freeing himself from the poverty of his past. Ironically, however, this road to freedom only put him in a worse position than if he had committed the petty robbery he originally planned. The Daltons may have meant well in their own way, but in the end, Bigger is found guilty and sentenced to die—a direct result of his association with the white family.

Native Son is not a happy story, but its powerful message makes it an important film. The characters are rich and complex. Bigger Thomas, in particular, is a haunting figure and one not easily forgotten. Through the story of this one character, author Wright succeeded in crystallizing the fear, tension, and brutality of racism. In many ways, the images he provoked created a disturbing picture—one that is always lingering, never resolved.

The Elements of Excellence

It is not possible to discuss the many great black films and talented performers in the course of this book. In part, this is because greatness remains a subjective and illusive quality. Its definition differs from one person to the next. And a film that has meaning to one particular group of people may fail to be a box-office success. Most people, however, would agree that certain objective criteria can be used to determine what sets an excellent film apart from the rest.

One such criterion is the historical relevance of the film. Does it have something new to say? Something that needed to be said? If the message is not new, does the film manage to get it across in a way that touches and moves the audience? Accuracy also plays an important role. How precisely does the movie portray the black experience? Was it merely a projection of a white person's perception of black America, or does it succeed in capturing an important aspect of reality?

A movie does not have to be a masterpiece to be great. When we examine the history of black Hollywood, the struggle of black artists to free themselves from the prevailing stereotypes cannot be ignored. Consequently, a film may be designated as great because one actor or actress gives a stellar, breakthrough performance, as do Paul Robeson in *Emperor Jones* and Sidney Poitier in *No Way Out*.

In addition to being well-made films that capture the audience's attention, the movies discussed here provide a unique insight into the "humanity" of the black experience. Black audiences left the theater feeling good about their heritage. Finally, here were some characters that departed from the usual one-dimensional stereotypes and roles subservient to a white superstar. Instead, the movies created real people with real emotions; people of depth and integrity.

By portraying the reality and the more uplifting aspects of the black experience, the movies enriched all Americans with a greater understanding and compassion. The films had something to say about what blacks have contributed to making America what it is today. In so doing, they added to our historical understanding of what makes a black person "real."

Mandela (TV, 1987): Danny Glover as Nelson Mandela

The Golden Child
(1986): Eddie Murphy
with Charlotte Lewis

Power (1986): Denzel Washington

Blue City (1986): Paul Winfield

Jumpin' Jack Flash
(1986): Whoopi Goldberg
with James Belushi

Street Smart (1987): Morgan Freeman with Christopher
Reeve

Big Shots (1987): Paul Winfield

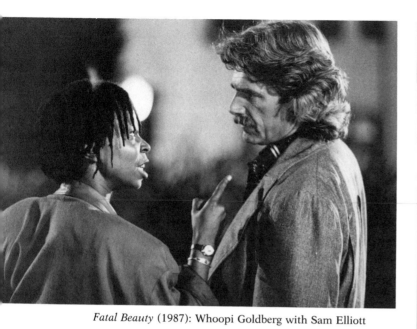

Fatal Beauty (1987): Whoopi Goldberg with Sam Elliott

Good Morning, Vietnam (1987): Forest Whitaker with Robin Williams

Gardens of Stone (1987): James Earl Jones with James Caan (left) and D. B. Sweeney

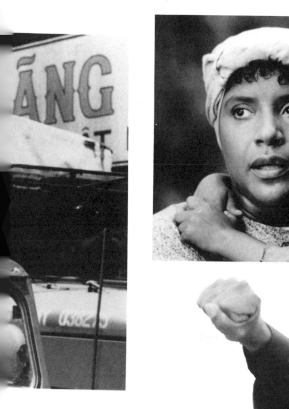

Uncle Tom's Cabin (TV, 1987): Phylicia Rashad and William Ramsey

Mandela (TV, 1987): Alfre Woodard as Winnie Mandela

The Offspring (1987): Rosalind Cash as the Snake
Woman

The Principal (1987): Louis Gossett Jr. with James
Belushi

Leonard Part 6 (1987):
Bill Cosby

172

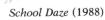 *Cry Freedom* (1987): Denzel Washington with Kevin Kline

School Daze (1988)

Shoot to Kill (1988): Sidney Poitier with Tom Berenger

Above the Law (1988): Pam Grier

Action Jackson (1988): Carl Weathers and Vanity

Bat-21 (1988): Danny Glover

Bird (1988): Forest Whitaker as Charlie "Bird" Parker

Deadly Intent (1988): Fred Williamson with Persis Khambatta

I'm Gonna Git You Sucka (1988): From left: Isaac Hayes, Bernie Casey, Keenen Ivory Wayans, and Jim Brown

Coming to America (1988): Eddie Murphy

176

Little Nikita (1988): Sidney Poitier with River Phoenix

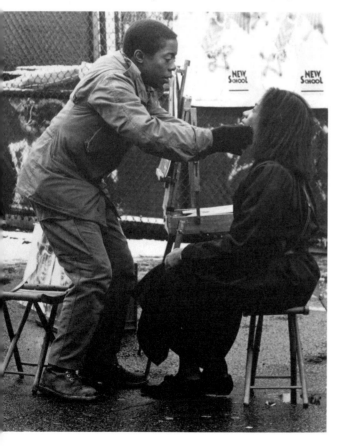

Tap (1988): Sammy Davis Jr. and Gregory Hines

Moving (1988): Beverly Todd and Richard Pryor

177

Sidewalk Stories (1989): Charles Lane and Sandye Wilson

Othello (1989): Ted Lange as director, executive producer, and star

Johnny Handsome (1989): Morgan Freeman

Snoops (TV, 1989): Tim and Daphne Reid

See No Evil, Hear No Evil (1989): Richard Pryor with Gene Wilder

178

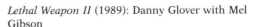

Lethal Weapon II (1989): Danny Glover with Mel Gibson

The Mighty Quinn (1989): Denzel Washington and Robert Townsend

The Mighty Quinn (1989): Tyra Ferrell and Robert Townsend

Do the Right Thing (1989): Spike Lee

6

The Rise of the Independents

Independent films, which are made outside the normal Hollywood structure, typically require a smaller budget than even the cheapest of mainstream productions. In some cases, an independent movie's low budget is painfully apparent. But in others, a well-written script and talented performers come together to make an excellent movie despite the absence of glitz. Oftentime, the uniqueness or importance of the film's message becomes the deciding factor in its success.

For people accustomed to Hollywood productions, independent films may appear to be flat. The difference between the two types of films is somewhat like that between Hollywood and Broadway. Younger Americans, in particular, who have been raised on television and fast-paced Hollywood movies, find it difficult to relate to live theater. It doesn't move fast enough, there isn't enough plot and action. The use of dance and song and intellectual themes may seem boring.

As a result, an independent filmmaker can expect a much smaller turnout than the studios generate. His or her productions may be identified as "art" or "cult" films, essentially ones that appeal to a particular audience rather than to the mass market. On the other hand, independents often work at the cutting edge of their profession. As relative newcomers to the field, they have high ideals and stay in touch with the reasons they chose to enter the business in the first place. For this reason, viewers who are tired of Hollywood's usual machinations may find independent films to be refreshing.

In the late 1980s, a wave of black independent filmmakers began to build. To many people, these writers and producers represent the hope of the future, not only in black filmmaking but in the black community itself. By functioning outside the established structure, independent filmmakers possess a freedom of expression that normally falls to a handful of moviemaking powerhouses. That freedom to be creative is an enormous advantage in Hollywood, which has become increasingly fossilized into a massive business enterprise.

Within that structure, the making of a quality film almost appears to be an accident.

Many critics also believe that Hollywood remains racist, offering little work for black actors, filmmakers, and technicians. Rather than chip away at well-entrenched attitudes, which wastes valuable energy, these artists believe it makes more sense to forge ahead on their own. With an independent film, one can also break away from the financial structure of major movies and work on a much lower budget. These days, most mainstream productions cost more than $15 million. As a result, studios generally want to make only those films that fall within proven categories, such as romantic comedies, adventure and action movies, and cops and robbers stories. Likewise, they may stick to films that feature star directors and performers.

This setup leaves little room for performers and directors who lack superstar credentials. It also leads to movies that are boring, uninspired, and utterly lacking in creativity. Therefore, an ambitious and dedicated artist with a message to convey may actually *prefer* to make an independent film, rather than view it as a vehicle of last resort. The independent arena offers those involved the freedom to express themselves creatively. It also provides actors with a chance to practice their craft without having to accept compromising roles. For the socially conscious black filmmaker, in fact, an independent production is a chance to put fellow artists to work.

In the 1980s, Spike Lee and Robert Townsend emerged as the most critically acclaimed black independent filmmakers. Before discussing the wave of independent films that followed in the 1990s, we will look at the trend where it started, with these two writer-directors.

Spike Lee

In his first three movies, released in the late 1980s, Spike Lee showed that he is a filmmaker with a firm dedication to "uplifting the race." While Lee served as producer, director, and actor, he also created meaningful roles for other black performers in films located exclusively in the black community, told from the black point of view, and aimed primarily at black audiences. A token white person may come onto the scene, but usually as a buffoon or a foil, much as blacks used to appear in Hollywood's earlier films. For many black viewers, this role reversal may come as a welcome relief: "Too long has the black man groveled at the feet of the white oppressor. Now it's time to see them squirm." In this regard, Lee's films serve as a catharsis of sorts, a means of liberation.

In many ways, Lee's work hints of better things to come for black America. He, personally, is a free man, not just from the vestiges of slavery but also from the Hollywood system. Lee is truly a free spirit, one who has chosen to make films and maintains total control of them as writer-producer-director-star, much like Woody Allen. He has set his ideals and forged ahead, snubbing his nose at compromise. The remarkable results of that mission, in the 1980s alone, were three critically acclaimed works in four years, following *Joe's Bed-Stuy: We Cut Heads*, the short film he made on a shoestring. *She's Gotta Have It*, *School Daze*, and *Do the Right Thing* were all independently produced movies that speak for and about black people. In this respect, Lee is indeed a powerful role model.

Lee's independence carries through to the message of the films as well. He focuses on the black experience, not in relationship to the white community or white ideals but as it stands on its own. By committing everyday scenes from a community such as Harlem to the screen, Lee gives the people living there validity and stature. This, in itself, is no small achievement. In these days of runaway poverty and homelessness, many social activists charge that America has forgotten about the so-called underclass. And if politicians who require votes overlook this population, how much truer is the accusation of Hollywood? In its quest for glamour, the moviemaking machinery almost instinctively shies away from the squalor, problems, and misery of the inner city. Lee's work makes an important contribution in this regard. He does not ignore the less savory facts of ghetto life, but he also reaches beyond them to create characters with whom the audience can largely identify.

The three films generally received good reviews from the critics. When the nominations were an-

She's Gotta Have It (1986): Writer, director, editor, and star Spike Lee

nounced for the 1989 Academy Awards, many film aficionadoes were surprised at the omission of *Do the Right Thing* although Danny Aiello was cited. But while some people blame racism for the Motion Picture Academy's oversight, others say it was racism in reverse that prevented the film from being great. Lee's contribution to "uplifting the race" also stirs hot debate. True, his day-in-the-life style of filming may play an important social role within the black community. But does he go far enough? Some film critics argue that the often angry Lee must depict more positive characters in his films if he truly wants to dedicate himself to improving the condition of black people.

In *Do the Right Thing* (1989), Lee presents a series of vignettes that portray life in the Bed-Stuy section of Brooklyn on a single hot summer day. The film opens to the rap song "Fight the Power," which laces throughout the movie to set the mood and underscore the message. Against a red backdrop, a young woman wearing boxing gloves punctuates the bass of the music with punches and hip thrusts. We see a storefront deejay who philosophizes on life as well as the weather. Through successive scenes, we then meet the film's other neighborhood denizens.

Apart from the police, there are only a handful of whites in the movie, with three painfully stereo-

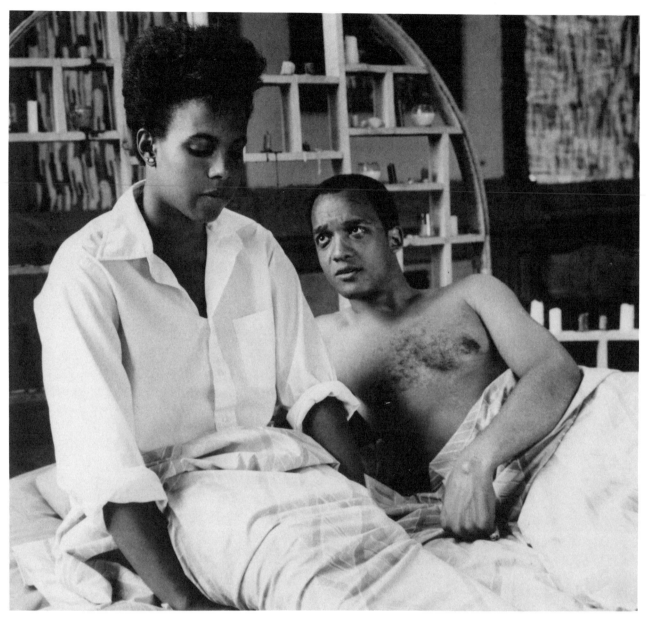

She's Gotta Have It (1986): Nola Darling and Jamie Overstreet

typed relatively uneducated Italians. Sal (Danny Aiello) owns Sal's Famous Pizzeria in what once was an Italian neighborhood. His two sons, Pino (John Turturro) and Vito (Richard Edson), work with him at the store. Lee uses these characters as indicative of whites in general. One son is an outright bigot who tries to talk his father into selling the pizzeria. "I'm sick of blacks," he says. "My friends laugh at me." The other does not appear to be outwardly racist. He never says anything offensive, but is portrayed as somewhat

mentally deficient, so his opinions are probably irrelevant anyway.

Sal himself vacillates between being a bigot and a good guy. He tells Pino that he's "never had no trouble with these people." At times, he is even paternalistic and nostalgic about the now all-black neighborhood. "This neighborhood grew up on my food," he says. But when pushed, Sal becomes as violently and vocally racist as anyone.

Lee plays the main character, Mookie, who works as a delivery boy at Sal's. Mookie's girlfriend

184

is the same young woman we saw dancing at the beginning of the film, a Puerto Rican black, probably about eighteen and the mother of Mookie's child. Like many characters in the film, both her accent and her language seem transplanted directly from the ghetto to the screen. In one scene, she has a screaming fight with her mother and then retires to her room in a muttering rage. ". . . makes me sick. Papa, too. He makes me sick. Everybody makes me sick. Shit. My father ain't no real father. He's a bum."

The other characters are equally distinctive. Smiley, a mentally retarded man, stutters as he tries to sell pictures of Malcolm X and Martin Luther King. Meanwhile, three middle-aged "schmoozers" hang out against a red wall and provide an on-going dialogue. "F--- Mike Tyson," says one. "Mike Tyson ain't shit." "And you gonna tell him that?" asks another. "Shur, I say f--- Mike Tyson. To his face," answers the first.

"Mother-Sister (Ruby Dee)," an older black woman, sits mournfully—and somewhat aggressively—at her window every day, watching the street life go by. The elderly "Mayor" (Ossie Davis) wanders the neighborhood doing good deeds whenever he gets the chance. And finally, there is "Bed-Stuy" or "Radio Raheem" (Bill Nunn), aptly named because he carries the biggest and loudest blaster in the neighborhood. The camera invariably captures "Radio" through an upward-pointing, wide-angle lens, distorting his features and giving him a surreal, larger-than-life look. His blaster plays the "Fight the Power" tune we hear throughout the movie. In one scene, "Radio" wages a "battle of noise" with a group of kids—he wins. But in the end, as we will see, it is also his noise that gets him killed.

Through interwoven clips of the various characters, we get a flavor of Bed-Stuy on a hot and steamy summer day. Sal opens the pizzeria, Mookie comes to work. When a neighborhood kid, "Buggin' Out" (Giancarlo Esposito), walks in for a slice, he notices that all the photographs on Sal's walls are of Italians—Al Pacino, Gina Lollobrigida, Frank Sinatra. "Why no brothers on the wall? he asks. Sal tells the kid that when he opens his own place, he can hang whatever pictures he likes on the wall. Outraged, the kid tries to organize a boycott of Sal's pizzeria, but no one in the

neighborhood will participate. Where else are they going to eat?

Finally, the kid joins forces with "Radio," who's already at odds with Sal who makes him turn off his blaster every time he enters the pizzeria—a violation of "Radio's" freedom of speech. The two barge into the pizzeria, one demanding brothers on the wall, the other cranking up his radio full volume. Sal argues with the two and then goes berserk. He takes a baseball bat to the radio and smashes it to pieces. The music dies out in a sickly drone, and then the real riot begins. Mookie instigates it by throwing a garbage can through Sal's window; the pizzeria is then looted and destroyed. The police arrive and struggle with "Radio," strangling him with a billy club choke hold. The film closes as Smiley hangs pictures of Malcolm X and Martin Luther King on the wall of what's left of Sal's place, accompanied by the beat of "Fight the Power."

Do the Right Thing has generated a lot of debate, with people weighing in on both sides about its merit. On the positive side, the movie does an excellent job of portraying a certain type of reality. Spike Lee creates true-to-life characters—in their speech, their mannerisms, and their reactions to the environment in which they live. Likewise, the film contains no heroes, no all-together good guys. Lee's character, Mookie, probably comes closest to being a hero. He has a fairly simpatico personality, holds down a regular job, is moderately diligent, gets along fairly well with Sal, at least up to his sudden act of defiance, and even elicits a confidential heart-to-heart talk with one of Sal's sons.

But Mookie also initiates the riot that destroys Sal's place and then shows no remorse for his actions. He even goes to Sal afterward to demand his wages. While no particular attention was paid to it in the movie, Mookie also makes a pretty poor excuse for a father. When he manages a "quickie" with his girlfriend between pizza deliveries, we learn only as an aside that Mookie is the father of her child. This cursory mention provides a pretty clear indication of the importance Mookie places on his role as a father.

The rest of the characters follow the same pattern, revealing both good and bad qualities. Sal, for example, seems to be a reasonably decent guy, once he gets past the uneducated Italian stereotype. But when he loses his temper, he says some inflammatory things and indirectly, at least, causes "Radio's" death. "Radio," for his part, was primarily a sympathetic character. With the blaster at his side, he only wanted to be heard and to be free to express himself.

Symbolically, "Radio" presents some profound issues. As the Supreme Court has argued, an individual's right of self expression must be weighed against the social costs. In this case, the noise pollution in major urban areas. But what if loud music means different things to different groups of people? Sal was annoyed and then outraged by "Radio's" music. The rest of the neighborhood, on the other hand, seemed to enjoy if not admire the street music. Depending on one's point of view, "Radio" may in fact have been a faultless victim.

This leads to the issue of racism, which was brilliantly addressed in the movie. While Lee may be an advocate of separatism—keeping the race pure—he also recognizes the universality of racism. In one scene, people of all races and ethnicity spew libelous slurs at other groups—Orientals against blacks, Catholics against Jews, black against white. We see virtually every imaginable combination of bigotry. Through this exchange, Lee aptly makes the point that all people, even those who consider themselves to be free of prejudice, resort to it in one form or another.

The character of Sal illustrates this point most clearly. For the most part, one feels that Sal truly likes or at least tolerates the people in the neighborhood that used to be "his" and even forgets about the black-white issue most of the time. Yet when pushed to the edge, Sal starts on a "Nigger" tirade. Once those words have been spoken, they cannot be withdrawn. One can easily conclude that the "real" Sal is a bigot and that his everyday face is merely a hypocrisy.

The strong points of *Do the Right Thing*, however, are also among its most glaring shortcomings. The film presents its story as *cinema verité*, for example, as if the images Lee captures are accurate portrayals of "reality." Certainly, the movie contains some realistic characters, but Lee's point of view is highly selective. Do all blacks, or at least all young black men living in Bed-Stuy, wear high-topped tennis shoes, baggy shorts over bicycle tights, and oversize shirts? Do they all use the same jivey sort of street language, liberally peppered with "shit," "f---" and "motherf---er"? Is sex really such a casual thing as it appears to be for Mookie and his girlfriend?

Lee does succeed in capturing certain glimpses of reality, but his vision hardly reflects the way in which the majority of black people go about their daily lives. Rather than stand as an image of black America, Lee's characters glorify a certain segment of the population. And by focusing on that particular segment, some critics charge, Lee perpetuates stereotypes that do little to advance his purported objective of "uplifting the race."

The use of stereotypes in black films is a complex and ambiguous issue. Hollywood has long been criticized for the paucity of rich and meaningful roles available to black artists. Critics claim that its pervasive racism makes it incapable of seeing black people as anything other than stereotypes. Yet here is Spike Lee, an independent (East Coast) filmmaker and a proclaimed social activist, doing precisely the same thing. The message is indeed confusing, particularly since his characters portray many of the most demeaning aspects of the black stereotypes. Is Lee saying that blacks can stereotype (and degrade) each other, but that if whites do the same it amounts to "racism" (the notion that one's own ethnic stock is superior[19])?

Perhaps some degree of stereotyping is inherent in all filmmaking. In *Sounder*, for example, the main characters belong to a "poor, black Southern family"; in *Native Son*, Bigger Thomas certainly exhibits some characteristics that could be classified as stereotypical. But these figures still differ from those in Lee's productions. In the truly great films, the characters have a substance and purpose that allow them to rise above the stereotypes and become individuals. In *Do the Right Thing*, conversely, Lee's glorification of his stereotypes effectively locks in the characters. From a social perspective, the end result is a perpetuation of the status quo rather than a liberation from it.

Writer-director Lee's treatment of social issues proves even more troubling, in part because the films themselves are racist. Had a white person made *Do the Right Thing*, the movie would have

---

[19]American Heritage Dictionary, 27th edition

been pointed to as the worst kind of bigotry. The story contains nonblack characters who are empty and ridiculous, precisely the kind of roles many blacks claim they must play in Hollywood. Will repeating the errors of the past, even if revenge happens to be sweet, bring about a resolution to the problem? Consider the abused child. Does he find relief in ultimately becoming a child beater himself, or does true freedom result from breaking the pattern once and for all?

The film's plot also appears to be shortsighted. It is practically inconceivable that the same story could be told from a white perspective in this day and age. Imagine a black small-businessman in a white neighborhood whose clientele badgers him because he only puts pictures of blacks on his walls. True, he would be in a precarious position if he gave in to the provocation of a kid like "Radio." Still, it is difficult to imagine an audience feeling anything but sympathy for him if a bunch of white yahoos burned his business to the ground. Particularly to a tune such as "Fight the Power."

School Daze (1988), another of Lee's films, also explores the issue of racism but from an all-black perspective. The story focuses on the problems between light-skinned and dark-skinned blacks rather than between blacks and whites. Set at Mission College, an all-black Southern university, the movie uses sororities and fraternities to symbolize various black "clans" and the ways in which they interact.

Faction #1, the social activists, is led by a dynamic intellectual named Dap (Larry Fishburne) who rails against the college's investment in South Africa at a time when other universities like Harvard and Yale have already divested. He is vehemently opposed to the concept of fraternities and sororities. Dap is black and proud of it; he believes in racial purity. He scoffs at those who grease down their hair, as if ashamed of their heritage.

Faction #2, the Gammites, is a trendy fraternity led by the fascistic Julian (Giancarlo Esposito), who reigns over the pledges like a military commander. He assigns them to perform all kinds of lewd and demeaning acts. Lee himself appears as a Gammite pledge, Darryl, a.k.a. "Half Pint." The pledges wear black-and-silver outfits that resemble spacesuits, complemented by goggles and shaven heads.

Faction #3, the Gamma Rays, is a sorority of snobby, light-skinned black girls. It is led by Jane (Tisha Campbell), a red-haired beauty and the girlfriend of Julian, while faction #4 consists of the dark-skinned girls. One of them, Rachel, is Dap's girlfriend.

Lee produced *School Daze* as a musical. And oddly enough, this approach to exploring racial tensions works quite well. The music and dance not only lighten the brutality of the racial epithets but also provide them with a dramatic intensity. In a number of scenes, for example, the two groups of girls clash, chanting their slurs as they dance to well-choreographed numbers. The dark-skinned girls taunt the others for choosing to dye their hair, use straighteners, and be neither black nor white. "You're not white, Your hair's only that way because you pull at it all night," they say. The light-skinned girls respond, "You belong in a zoo. Jigaboo. Jigaboo."

In addition to the issue of skin color, the movie explores a broad range of dilemmas facing black Americans today. Indeed, Lee does a remarkable job of addressing the following issues:

• Class: In one scene, Dap and his friends go into town to eat at the Kentucky Fried Chicken. There, they come up against the "Townies," a group of older, uneducated men who have lived there all of their lives. The two groups challenge each other outside. The "Townies" complain that the college students are arrogant and stuck up, that they have taken over the town and that they don't belong there. The students retort with a verbal attack on the men: "Why are you wearing all those chemicals in your hair. Wearing a shower cap like a bitch. Nigger. You'll always be niggers."

• Roots: Dap and Julian conflict at many levels, particularly in their perceptions of what it means to be "black." Dap takes pride in being 100 percent black; he can trace his roots. He is an Afro-American, with more emphasis on the Afro than on the American. He also dislikes fraternities because they encourage conformity rather than individuality. Julian, on the other hand, not only leads a fraternity but makes no bones about saying he is from Detroit, from "Motown!" He tells Dap, "If you don't like it here, you can just

Watusi your black ass back to Africa. You don't know anything about Africa."

- Sexuality: While Lee's personal position on women may not be clear in the film, he most definitely exposes the black male machismo in *School Daze*. The light-skinned girls meow and whine like cats in the opening scene. When the Gammites deign to invite them to the frat house, the girls must first agree to clean the place. Later, as a condition of pledging, Darryl must "find a woman" and prove that he is not a virgin. He asks a fraternity brother what he should say to his female candidates. The response: "Tell them whatever they want to hear."

In one of the only scenes in which the women show their intelligence, we watch as a straight-faced Darryl tries to convince one girl after another to go out with him. They all turn him down. But not to worry. Julian solves the problem by offering Darryl his own girlfriend, the voluptuous Jane. He wanted to get rid of Jane anyway, it seems. Darryl and Jane spend a number of hours together in the "bone room." When Jane emerges, she is totally humiliated. She says she went through with it only because she believed Julian wanted her to. But Julian feigns incomprehension, leaving Jane to feel that she is a worthless slut.

Overall, the movie is remarkably well done. Lee shows particular insight when it comes to revealing the many ways in which human beings can degrade and humiliate each other. And *School Daze*, unlike *Do the Right Thing*, ends with a positive message. When Dap discovers what has happened to Jane, he races across the campus in a rage, yelling "Wake Up" over and over again. Eventually, he manages to arouse the entire facility, which assembles in the quad and stands at attention. The film closes as Dap pleads, "Please, wake up."

Robert Townsend

With his first film, *Hollywood Shuffle* (1987), filmmaker Robert Townsend drew wide critical acclaim. In addition to being utterly hilarious, the movie offers a brilliant exposé on the dilemmas young black actors face in Hollywood. Like Lee's films, *Hollywood Shuffle* was an independent production. Townsend coauthored (with Keenen Ivory Wayans), produced, directed, and starred in the movie as Bobby Taylor, an aspiring young actor.

As the film opens, Taylor is rehearsing a ridiculous role from a movie script, using a whiny, high-pitched voice. The handsome, vibrant, enthusiastic, well-rounded Taylor lives at home with his mother, grandmother, and younger brother, and also works part-time at a diner called the "Winky-Dinky Dog," where he sells hotdogs and wears a paper cap that has weenies stuck to it like horns. Yes, actor-director Townsend has a real sense of humor.

As the movie progresses, we see the trials and tribulations black actors experience as movie hopefuls. At one point, Taylor goes to an audition for which he has an appointment. When he arrives on time and announces his name to the receptionist, he is told to take a seat—among a throng of other applicants. Without words, Taylor conveys not only his own disappointment but also the cruel realities faced by most young actors in Hollywood. This was *his* appointment. He held up his end of the bargain—rehearsing his lines, arriving on time, being dedicated to this career. Yet he is asked to forget his pride and dignity—to take a number and shut up.

The implication is that Taylor should be grateful to be there at all. He at least has an agent with enough clout to get him in the front door of a studio, which is more than one can say for the many poor slobs who can't even get past an agent's secretary. Taylor is young and innocent, but if he "makes it," will he remain that way for long? He is an individual with real emotions, while Hollywood is a massive machine. Its only interest in the Bobby Taylors of the world lies in whether or not it can mold them to its purposes.

Taylor takes his seat. Another young black, obviously auditioning for the same part, sits down next to him and bad-mouths the script. "It's the white man's stereotype. Don't belittle yourself by doing these roles," he tells Taylor, implying that *he* would never stoop so low. The actor then prances off to his own audition. Later in the film, the audience's suspicions about the self-righteous actor are confirmed. When Taylor subsequently

Hollywood Shuffle (1987): Robert Townsend (left), Keenen Ivory Wayans (center), and John Witherspoon

walks off the set, resigning his hard-won role, the other actor is the first to grab at it.

The issue of compromise runs throughout the film. The part for which Taylor rehearses is a stupidly vapid character, and he must compromise his dignity by waiting in line for hours for the "privilege" of auditioning. The repulsive nature of the three white producers, who symbolize all of Hollywood, only compounds the humiliation. Crass, insensitive, and totally uncultured, the producers have no compunction about exploiting the innocence and desperation of striving young actors. In a series of scenes, we see the three interviewing various hopefuls. What they ask of them is demeaning and unreasonable. They want someone who is tough, but sensitive; cruel, but compassionate; street-smart, but innocent; mean, but appealing. When Taylor auditions, they tell him they want an "Eddie Murphy type." Taylor asks what that means, and the producers respond, "Well, you know. We want you to act like Eddie Murphy." (Ironically, Townsend would go on to next direct *Eddie Murphy Raw*.)

Taylor eventually lands the part, only to discover the true meaning of compromise. As part of a prestigious Hollywood production, Taylor finds himself among the chosen few. But at what price? Both his role and the movie are a complete farce. On location, we see a collection of grotesque, buffoon-like characters, all shufflin', jivin', and shooting each other. Taylor enters the scene in a beige pimp suit and bouffant wig. He tries to deliver his lines in the whiny voice, but eventually faces reality. He can never feel good about playing such a character. It demeans him personally and openly assaults his race. Dejected, he walks off the set. But his integrity is still intact.

Part of Townsend's charm as a filmmaker lies in his delightful sense of humor. He has the ability to take an emotionally charged issue, such as the stereotyping of blacks, and expose it through wit instead of anger. As Taylor waits in line for his audition, he contemplates what the other actor has said and begins to daydream about the limited possibilities for black actors. Suddenly, a ridiculous parody of a Southern slave drama fills the

189

screen. As a handsome runaway slave creeps from his hiding place, a Southern belle appears. She begs the slave to take her with him, claiming that life on the plantation has become unbearable.

The film then cuts to an immaculately clad Taylor. Speaking in a proper British accent, he advertises the "first all-black acting school in the country." With a tongue-in-cheek cool, Taylor promises young hopefuls that they, too, can learn to play slaves, street thugs, and pimps. But only dark-skinned blacks need apply, mind you. The name of the school then flashes across the screen, along with details of the vast possibilities: Learn to play street pimps, movie muggers, slaves, and prostitutes. Classes offered include: "Jive Talk 101," "Shuffling 200," and "Epic Slaves 400." For information, dial 1-800-555-COON.

In another spoof about black roles, we see the character of "Batty Boy," a black television superstar humorously modeled after *Batman*. In one of the television scenes, Batty Boy arrives in a white stretch limo, complete with bodyguards, at the Winky-Dinky Dog. When Taylor and his coworkers serve Batty Boy, they are in awe of the grandeur that stands before them. Taylor confides to Batty Boy that he too hopes to be a great actor one day. In response, Taylor is offered a piece of profound wisdom. "It's not about art," Batty Boy says. "It's about sequel. One film can make your career."

Hollywood Shuffle's title is apropos on every level: There's the shuffling that takes place during the auditioning, filmmaking, and distributing of the finished product. The competition among young actors. The struggle to make a living while pursuing one's career. Shuffling to the top, shuffling at the top, shuffling on down to the bottom again. In a particularly funny passage, Townsend even captures the "Shuffle of the Critics." As Taylor and his friends play basketball, they agree that blacks need their own critics—a Siskel and Ebert for "the brothers." Here, Taylor lapses into another dream sequence, this one featuring him and a friend in a parody of Siskel and Ebert. The two sneak into a theater. Taylor introduces himself as "Spin" and his partner as his "homeboy, Tyrone." "We're like movie critics and shit," says Spin. The two then review *Amadeus*, which Spin tells us is about "two motherf---ers really into music." Tyrone's review: "Bullshit. I didn't like that movie.

My first problem was that I couldn't say the title. I get tired of titles I can't pronounce and shit. If you want people to move and see it, a motherf---er gotta be able to tell his woman where he's gonna take her."

The two also pan a "Chicago Jones" and "Dirty Larry" because the movies are too unrealistic. They do, however, agree that "Attack of the Street Pimps" is a great success. A clip of the movie shows prostitutes cowering in a corner as a mob of ghoulish pimps stalk the streets. "Motherf---er scared the shit out of me, man," says Spin. "That shit can really happen." Adds Tyrone: "I believe this movie. Like you get all those pimps together, walkin' around and shit, whith those big hats on . . . Yeah, the director captured the essence of street life in whore-type situation."

Finally, the morass of conflicting ideals and realities within the black community is yet another "shuffle." As an aspiring actor, Taylor needs roles and he needs to get his name noticed. Otherwise, he will never get anywhere. He probably has to start at the bottom and work his way to the top, but the bottom for most young actors (not only blacks) means roles that are frivolous or outright degrading.

When Taylor has second thoughts about his role, he has a dream in which everyone—his mother, friends, even his brother and girlfriend—turn against him for becoming a success. An NAACP spokesperson also denounces Taylor. "Black actors should not have to take these roles. They'll never play the Rambos until they stop playing the Sambos."

The movie's conclusion makes a sad statement about Hollywood. Dignity and integrity, it seems, are incompatible with the hard realities of the film industry. After Taylor gives up the demeaning role, he abandons acting and goes to work for the post office. There, at least, he finds work that allows him to live as a human being. The film ends there, with the fundamental choice Taylor makes: "To Be or Not to Be."

William Greaves

No discussion of black independent filmmakers would be complete without some examination of their impact upon our social consciousness. In this respect, one—William Greaves—stands out.

190

Greaves not only had a unique career in the cinema but also has made profound and prolific contributions to the field.

Beginning as an actor in the 1940s, in movies such as *Miracles in Harlem* and *Lost Boundaries,* Greaves went on to distinguish himself in stage, radio, television, and even as a dancer. He has written more than one hundred songs, including "African Lullaby." He also appeared in the original Broadway production of *Finian's Rainbow* and has been a performer with the American Negro Theater. But Greaves's greatest contribution was as executive producer and cohost of the first black nationally-aired public affairs television series, *Black Journal,* for which he won an Emmy Award. The socially conscious filmmaker produced more than eight episodes of the show.

From the 1960s to the 1980s, Greaves served as a writer, editor, cameraman, director, or producer for more than two hundred films. He has received more than forty-five international awards and owns the most succesful independent black film production studio in the United States. The company, which he started in 1964, has consistently earned recognition from national and international film viewers. Among its many outstanding films is *From These Roots,* which won more than twenty festival awards and serves as a classic in Afro-American history studies.

William Greaves Productions not only makes documentaries, television programs, and feature films, but also distributes library films and videotapes for television, educational institutions, corporations, and other users. His documentary films have been narrated or hosted by such names as Bill Cosby, Bob Hope, Anthony Quinn, Phylicia Rashad, Harry Belafonte, Ricardo Montalban, Marie Osmond, Rita Moreno, Brock Peters, and Gil Noble.

Greaves also participated in the "Films of the Civil Rights" series, which was presented by Joseph Papp's Public Theater in 1989. He was executive producer of *Bustin' Loose* (1981), starring Richard Pryor and Cicely Tyson; *Marijuana Affair;* and *Ali, the Fighter,* starring Muhammad Ali and Joe Frazier. In the early nineties, he directed and produced with Paul Robeson Jr. and Joseph Papp a Broadway celebration of Paul Robeson's ninetieth birthday.

I've found William Greaves to be a unique and humble man. All who know him recognize that he is a consummate professional who cares deeply about the quality of his work. He is dedicated to broadening our understanding of the black experience through the American cinema.

Lean on Me (1989):
Morgan Freeman

Driving Miss Daisy (1989): Morgan Freeman with Jessica
Tandy

The Price of the Ticket (TV, 1989): Maya Angelou and producer Bill Miles with coproducer-director Karen Thorsen

Katherine Anne Porter's *The Witness* (TV, 1989): Paul Winfield with Dina Chandel

Graffiti Bridge (1990): Prince as writer, director, and star

The Long Walk Home (1990): Whoopi Goldberg with Lexi Randall

El Diablo (TV, 1990):
Louis Gossett Jr.

*The Josephine Baker
Story* (TV, 1991): Lynn
Whitfield

A Rage in Harlem (1991): Forest Whitaker and Robin Givens

Star Trek VI: The Undiscovered Country (1991): Nichelle Nichols as Uhura with *Starship Enterprise* crewmates (from left) Walter Koenig, George Takai, DeForest Kelley, William Shatner, James Doohan, and Leonard Nimoy

Grand Canyon (1991): Danny Glover and Alfre Woodard

Ricochet (1991): Denzel
Washington with John
Lithgow

The Last Boy Scout (1991): Damon Wayans with Bruce
Willis

Strictly Business (1991): Joseph C. Phillips, Halle Berry, and Tommy Davidson

Pastime (1991): Glenn Plummer with
William Russ

House Party! (1991): Christopher Reid and
Tisha Campbell

New Jack City (1991): Ice-T with Judd Nelson

7
Into the Nineties

The success of Spike Lee and Robert Townsend finally accomplished the inevitable: The Hollywood establishment recognized that movies relating the black experience would attract a mixed, middle-class audience. As a result, the studios started snapping up scripts by and about blacks. In 1991 alone, nineteen movies by black directors were scheduled for release. The media noted the about-face in Hollywood with articles such as "They Gotta Have Us" in the *New York Times Magazine*, which explored the potential impact of this new phenomenon on the Hollywood system and on the black filmmaking community itself.[20]

By summer, four of the films had hit the theaters and a common perspective was taking shape. All four—*Boyz N the Hood, Jungle Fever, Straight Out of Brooklyn,* and *New Jack City*—marked a return to the slice-of-life films that had not been seen since the 1950s. Several of them are reminiscent of

The Education of Sonny Carson, a stark portrayal of what it means to be a young black growing up in a tough urban neighborhood, where enormous peer pressure forces many blacks to adopt a streetwise life-style.

In the past, however, moviegoers saw a sanitized version of the black perspective created by white directors. Today's black directors shift that viewpoint dramatically to give audiences a realistic, visceral, often gritty look at topics such as domestic violence, the effect of drugs on black neighborhoods, the cultural tragedy of blacks killing blacks, and interracial romance. While the new movies vary in theme and tone, all show some aspect of the price our society pays for its indifference to the needs of the urban black. The portrayal of some young people, in particular, reveals the tremendous effort it takes to transcend a debilitating environment. These children must overcome not only racism and street violence but also a lack of education, adult role models, and emotional nurturing.

---

[20]Bates, Karen Grigsby, "They Gotta Have Us," *New York Times Magazine,* July 14, 1991, p. 15

Livin' Large! (1991): Lisa Arrindell, T. C. Carson, and Nathaniel "Afrika" Hall

The movies' leading actors also signal a departure from the past. The likes of Jim Brown and Fred Williamson, the superstars of the 1970s black exploitation films, are nowhere to be seen. Nor do the films feature the romantic, crossover type artists who either achieved star power in the 1980s or reemerged from an earlier period, such as Danny Glover, Denzel Washington, Louis Gossett Jr., Sidney Poitier, and Billy Dee Williams. For the most part, the stars of these films are young and relatively unknown men and women who represent today's lower- and middle-class blacks as they truly exist, thereby giving the movies a fresh and contemporary look.

The box office results, especially considering the lack of big-name stars, were nothing short of phenomenal. Never in movie history have four black films run concurrently and raked in such huge ticket sales. By year's end, the movies had a combined income of some $165 million. *Boyz N the Hood*, in particular, generated $45.4 million in its first six weeks alone, outpacing all but a few

other films in its weekly box-office sales. Clearly, moviegoers of all types—black and white, across the social classes—are drawn to realistic portrayals of blacks in today's society.

The Good, the Bad, and the Reality

Boyz N the Hood opened to the kind of reviews that make for Hollywood legend. It was hailed as "Academy Award material," "a remarkable debut film," and "a powerhouse movie . . . the work of a truly gifted filmmaker." John Singleton, the twenty-three-year-old writer and director, tells a rich and moving story from a viewpoint that moviegoers rarely experience: A lower-class black teenager coming of age in a rough Los Angeles neighborhood.

It begins with a startling message: One of every twenty-one black American males will die before reaching adulthood, most killed by another black male. The theme of ghetto violence, of blacks killing blacks, runs throughout the film, which focuses on the lives of three teenagers. Tre Styles (Cuba Gooding Jr.) has divorced but caring parents who are determined to provide him with the right moral and educational input. His best friends, however, brothers Ricky (Morris Chestnut) and Doughboy (Ice Cube), are being raised by a single mother (Tyra Ferrell) who has little to offer along those lines. She treats her children inconsistently, with affection for Ricky and disregard for Dough-boy.

A Raisin in The Sun was the first black film which strongly demonstrated the importance of concerned and loving parenting. In the years following we had *The Learning Tree, Sounder, Sounder II,* and *Claudine.* But *Boyz N the Hood* blazed new trails. When a young Tre first goes to live with his father, he learns that he will have rules to follow and someone to whom he must answer at all times. Tre's father, Furious Styles (Larry Fishburne) projects the movie's outcome when he tells Tre that Doughboy and Ricky aren't so lucky because no one is teaching them about responsibility. "You'll see how they turn out," he says.

That prophecy pans out soon enough. By the time the boys are in high school, Tre has matured into a responsible young man who works part-time in a clothing store and plans to attend college. His relationship with his girlfriend is based on love and respect, not just sexual attraction. Ricky, too, has fared relatively well. Although he has become a father at a very young age, he is a talented football player who hopes to receive a college scholarship. Doughboy, however, has already been in and out of trouble with the law. He spends his days just hanging out, a recipe for trouble. He also carries a gun.

Eventually, the random and chronic violence that pervades the neighborhood reaches these three friends, who have formed close emotional ties. When a local gang member deliberately bumps into Ricky, Doughboy overreacts in a typical tough-guy manner by pulling his gun. The gang later retaliates by gunning down Ricky in the streets. The movie makes its point: To see a sweet and promising young man killed is tragic indeed. Yet as the opening message states, it happens all the time.

In the end, *Boyz N the Hood* draws a telling contrast between teenagers like Tre who receive firm parental guidance and those such as Dough-boy who drift aimlessly in the cultural morass. When Tre, Doughboy, and two other friends go out to find the gang members and avenge Ricky's death, Tre suddenly tells Doughboy to stop the car and let him out. At that moment, Tre chooses his own future and his father's way over the satisfaction of revenge. Whether consciously or not, he also chooses not to become a part of the cycle in which blacks kill blacks.

Doughboy, conversely, makes the opposite choice. When he finds the three gang members, one of his friends shoots them down, injuring but not killing two of them. Doughboy jumps out of the car and shoots one of the two instinctively, the other deliberately. Again, whether consciously or not, he has become a part of the vicious cycle. The next day, Doughboy tells Tre that he doesn't know how he feels about what happened. "This shit just goes on and on," he says. "The next thing someone might try to smoke me." The movie ends there, but title cards tell us that Doughboy is killed a few

Livin' Large! (1991): Director Michael Schultz

weeks later and that Tre and his girlfriend leave for college, triumphing over their environment.

The movie points to racism as the real culprit in this cycle of killing. At one point, Furious Styles tells Tre and Ricky that white society "wants us to kill outselves." As evidence, he points to the proliferation of gun and liquor shops in black neighborhoods. But to pin the blame strictly on whites is to ignore the reality of the larger social context. After all, many whites are also poor, many are alcoholics and drug addicts, and many own guns as well. Meanwhile, white and black merchants alike sell these dangerous commodities for the same reason cigarettes and other harmful products are sold—there's a big profit to be made. It's more likely that the people pushing guns and liquor just don't care about the consequences, not that they actually want a certain segment of the population to die.

In *Straight Out of Brooklyn,* similar themes are brought to light but on a smaller scale. Nineteen-year-old writer-producer-director Matty Rich reportedly made the film on a budget of less than $100,000. In the past, the film may not have made it into the theaters due to its lack of technical merit. But in today's environment, the movie has done quite well. It drew box-office sales of more than $2.4 million in its first thirteen weeks, while playing on only sixty screens.

Rich's protagonist is a black teenager named Dennis (Lawrence Gilliard Jr.) who lives in a housing project in the Red Hook section of Brooklyn. Dennis's father, Ray (George T. Odom), is an abusive alcoholic who routinely vents his rage at "the white man" by beating his wife, Frankie (Ann Sanders), and verbally abusing Dennis and his sister. In the opening scene, one of rough domestic violence, we see that Ray, a frustrated gas station attendant who had dreamed of becoming a doctor, is a man who feels emasculated because he cannot materialize his own goals and become the ultimate provider for his family.

Ray appears to live his life as a trapped animal, caught not only by the reality of racism but also by his own anger and his inability to overcome the oppression in any positive way. He certainly behaves like an animal when he beats his wife, who continues to defend him in an effort to hold the family together. Ray's victimization has an enormous impact on Dennis, who believes that some

quick and easy money would solve his problems and get him out of Brooklyn. When his girlfriend, Shirley (Reana E. Drummond), accuses him of seeking the easy way out, Dennis responds that there is no wrong way out of their kind of neighborhood. "I don't want to live like animals anymore," he says.

Dennis tells his best friends, Larry (writer-director Rich himself) and Kevin (Mark Malone), that he "wants to get paid" like everyone else, but that he doesn't want to take the slow route of working in a gas station (as his father does). He asks them to help him rob some drug dealers who deliver money in the neighborhood every week, and his friends eventually agree. They plan and commit

Boyz N the Hood (1991): Ice Cube

202

the crime, but Dennis's friends then decide they don't want the money.

His response to his problems is complex. What appears to be a purely lazy solution, stealing money, also represents a desperate attempt to change the hostile environment in which he lives. While a college education would indeed improve his future, it won't solve the immediate everyday problems. It won't stop the pain he feels, it won't keep his father from beating his mother, and it won't make them a functional family. With no support system to help him overcome these problems, it's not so surprising that Dennis thinks money will do the trick.

But the very solution that he believes will liber-ate him from the trap only leads to more destruction. When Dennis brings the stolen money home, his father reacts violently and pushes his mother to the floor. She later dies in a hospital. At the same time, the drug dealers ripped off by Dennis chase his father down and shoot him. The movie ends abruptly as the gun shots ring out. Unlike *Boyz N the Hood,* in which the protagonist makes it out of the neighborhood, the film does not tell us what happens to Dennis.

Spike Lee's 1991 film, *Jungle Fever,* also explores the issue of racism, but from another angle entirely, focusing on interracial romance and the consequences for those who become involved in such relationships. From Lee's perspective, it seems, it is based more on curiosity about the other race than on mutual love or respect. Through most of the movie's characters, both black and white, Lee makes a negative statement about mixed relationships.

But the interracial couple he presents barely stands a chance. Flipper Purify (Wesley Snipes) is a professional black man from Harlem, an archi-tect in a white-owned Manhattan firm and a

Boyz N the Hood (1991): Larry Fishburne

devoted husband and father. Angie (Annabella Sciorra) comes from a similar social class but a very distinct world. She is a young, single Italian-American woman who lives with her father and brothers in Bensonhurst, a Brooklyn neighborhood that has come to symbolize racial intolerance. Angie goes to work as Flipper's secretary; the two become attracted and begin an affair.

When the news gets out, Flipper and Angie must contend with the angry reactions of their families and friends. Flipper's wife, Drew (Lonette McKee), kicks him out of the house. While her anger is understandable, she seems to feel more betrayed by Flipper's involvement with a white woman than by his infidelity in general. Angie, meanwhile, faces even more drastic consequences. When her father learns that she is seeing a black man, he beats her severely. She too must leave home.

While a few people on each side of the affair defend interracial romance, most of the characters disapprove strongly. Flipper's best friend, Cyrus, played by Spike Lee, calls the relationship a "nuclear holocaust." Flipper's father accuses Angie of fulfilling the fantasies originally held by white slave owners to sleep with "a big black buck." And some of Drew's friends attribute black men's fascination with "white things" strictly to a social-climbing desire to move up in the world. On

Boyz N the Hood (1991): Oscar-nominated writer and director John Singleton

Straight Out of Brooklyn (1991): Writer, producer, and director Matty Rich

Angie's side, nearly everyone expresses disgust at the very idea of a mixed relationship.

Flipper and Angie get an apartment together, but the relationship is ultimately doomed. While many interracial marriages are based on a strength and commitment in which color becomes secondary, we sense that these two will never overcome the dogmas of their disapproving families. Flipper tells Angie he does not love her and that their relationship was based purely on curiosity. But would he have gone to the trouble of moving in with her if he really felt nothing? More likely, he is consumed by guilt because he betrayed his wife and child. By denying that an emotion such as love exists, he does not have to take responsibility for it.

Lee displays a strong bias in the way he develops his characters. As in *Do the Right Thing*, he chooses an extremely narrow band of New York-bred Italians to represent the viewpoints of whites. The men who hang out at a neighborhood store run by Paulie (John Turturro), Angie's boyfriend before she meets Flipper, all come across as uneducated and vindictive in their conversations, especially Paulie's hot-headed father (Anthony Quinn). Ang-

Straight Out of Brooklyn (1991): Lawrence Gilliard Jr. and Reana E. Drummond

205

ie's family members, too, are single-dimensioned Italian-American caricatures. Only Flipper's bosses, who deny him a well-deserved promotion, provide a variation on the theme by portraying up-scale, crafty racists as opposed to the coarse Bensonhurst types.

The black characters, on the other hand, show much greater depth, variety, and humanistic qualities. Their witty, sophisticated, and intellectual conversations contrast sharply with that of the stereotyped Italians. Even the movie's subplot features fully drawn black characters. Three of the best roles, in fact, include Flipper's quirky parents (Ossie Davis and Ruby Dee) and his junkie brother, Gator (Samuel Jackson). The father is a self-righteous holy-roller who distances himself from his own children; the mother is a woman caught between her husband and her sons, trying to please both. In the end, the father shoots his son who has come to beg for drug money one too many times.

While *Jungle Fever* comes to an essentially distrustful conclusion about interracial romance, the movie contains less of the anger that fueled Lee's earlier ones, and it does match the others in its highly. stylized manner. Lee's films always look good, and they always make a controversial statement. Those qualities appeal to moviegoers across all racial and social lines. Like its predecessors, *Jungle Fever* was a financial success with box-office grosses of more than $35 million.

In *New Jack City*, Mario Van Peebles took a completely different approach to portraying life in the ghettos. In his first role as big-screen director, Van Peebles delivered a slick and fast-paced black gangster film that differs from the other three in both tone and content, following a group of young ghetto individuals who decide to do as much as they can to manipulate for fast dollars their own turf. But unlike the other movies, it is extraordinarily violent. And there are no good guys in this neighborhood.

Virtually all of the characters are part of a black drug and crime ring that exploits other blacks. The portrait of the ghetto is frightening and bleak—crack rings, nonstop violence, and the fast, hard life of drug dealers who dominate the neighborhood. The movie comes across as a black exploitation film, but one that is slicker and better directed, better acted and more sophisticated than any of its old counterparts. It is like a Steven Seagal film in its action; an urban *Rambo* in its violence. That combination clearly has appeal. *New Jack City* pulled in nearly $50 million on a budget of just $8.5 million.

8
The Black Experience Goes Mainstream

By 1992, slice-of-life films about black experiences in American society were less prominent than in the previous two years. Still, 1992 can only be called a huge success for black filmmakers and actors alike. In addition to the release of *Malcolm X*, Spike Lee's epic portrayal of the slain black leader, more than a dozen films either starring or costarring popular black actors came to the screen. With some notable exceptions, such as Eddie Murphy's *Boomerang*, many of these films were financial and critical successes.

In fact, black actors starred in some of the year's big blockbusters—Whoopi Goldberg in *Sister Act*, Danny Glover (with Mel Gibson) in *Lethal Weapon 3*, and Denzel Washington in *Malcolm X*. In addition, Sidney Poitier costarred in *Sneakers*, Morgan Freeman was in *Unforgiven*, and Whitney Houston made her acting debut in *The Bodyguard*. Some smaller but highly successful films also hit the

screen, including *White Men Can't Jump*, costarring Wesley Snipes, and *Juice*, the directorial debut of Ernest Dickerson, Spike Lee's longtime cinematographer.

Without a doubt, Hollywood has taken note of the financial prowess of some of these movies. In October 1992, *Variety* listed the ten most profitable films of the year according to the studios' return on investment (ROI). On that list: *Sister Act* (No. 3) with a 75 percent ROI; *Lethal Weapon 3* (No. 4) with a 37 percent ROI; *Juice* (No. 6) with a 36 percent ROI; and *White Men Can't Jump* (No. 10) with a 21 percent ROI.[21]

There's no denying that the figures generated by these titles, plus *The Body Guard*, *Passenger 57*, and *The Distinguished Gentleman*, are important to the black filmmaking community; they remind Hollywood that black actors can star in money-makers. But many of the films with box-office draw in 1992 were very different in tone and content from those that captured our attention in 1991. In fact, the emergence of black, inner-city

---

[21]Cohn, Lawrence, "Profits' the Thing, Not the Box Office Tally," *Variety*, October 5, 1992, p. 1.

films at the start of the nineties seemed to be usurped in 1992 by big Hollywood movies that paired black and white stars in combinations that would appeal to all audiences.

In keeping with Hollywood tradition, most of these screen partnerships featured men. The winning twosome of Danny Glover and Mel Gibson in *Lethal Weapon 3* was joined by the new combinations of Sidney Poitier and Robert Redford in *Sneakers*, Morgan Freeman and Clint Eastwood in *Unforgiven*, and Wesley Snipes and Woody ("Cheers") Harrelson in *White Men Can't Jump*. One movie, *The Bodyguard*, went against the grain by combining a white male lead, Kevin Costner, with a black female costar, Whitney Houston.

Beyond that, two colorblind movies in 1992 drew their comedic fuel from the placement of black leads in essentially all-white situations. In *Sister Act*, Whoopi Goldberg's street-wise character must hide out in a convent of white nuns. And in *The Distinguished Gentleman*, Eddie Murphy plays a con man elected to a largely white congress. By contrast, the films that featured black situations included *Boomerang*, which placed Eddie Murphy in the world of upwardly mobile black businesspeople, and *Juice*, a coming-of-age story set in Harlem. And then, of course, there was *Malcolm X*, another story entirely.

Malcolm X: A Landmark Film

With the making of *Malcolm X*, Spike Lee broke the mold of the black filmmaking genre. Unlike many black movies, which are independent productions with small budgets, Lee's *Malcolm X* was a big Hollywood production with a budget of some $40 million to match. With this film, Warners was betting that the story of a highly controversial black man—feared by many for the militancy of his message—would appeal to both black and white moviegoers.

In *Time* magazine, Lee acknowledged that the movie's success or failure would set a precedent for other black filmmakers in Hollywood: "[It] is going to be a big hit," he said, "and it's really going to crumble that old, tired Hollywood axiom that the white moviegoing masses are not going to see a black film that's a drama, or a film that's not a comedy or a musical, or that doesn't have Eddie Murphy in it. Because no matter what lip service

these executives say, that is still their belief."[22]

Malcolm X received an unusual amount of media attention from its inception to its release. First came Lee's wrestling match with Canadian-born director Norman Jewison over which of the two should film the story of Malcolm X. Jewison was set to do a movie himself, but Lee convinced him that only a black director could do justice to the life of one of the most important voices in African-American history. But no sooner had Lee gained control of the project than he was attacked by black artists such as playwright Amiri Baraka, (the erstwhile Leroi Jones) a Malcolm X colleague who claimed on behalf of the United Front to Preserve the Legacy of Malcolm X that Lee would produce a sanitized version of Malcolm X's life to make "middle-class Negroes sleep easier."[23]

The next publicity ruckus came during the editing of the film, when Lee went $5 million over budget and Warners refused to put up the extra cash. The bonding company that insured Warner Bros. against such an overrun had decided to cut off Lee's funding. Despite the fact that the film's guarantor is a black company, Lee attributed the episode to studio racism. "Warner Bros. didn't come up like they should have come up on this—pure and simple," stated Lee in a December 1992 interview with *Ebony*. "And they've come up for a lot of other garbage. But that's par for the course—they come up for White folks. They don't come up for us—ever."[24]

So Lee reached out to some of the richest black celebrities in America and immediately received money from the likes of Oprah Winfrey, Bill Cosby, Prince, and Magic Johnson. Following Lee's highly unusual—and painfully public—fund-raising mission, Warner Bros. began to supply more money as well.

And finally, the release of *Malcolm X* itself was accompanied by a tremendous amount of media attention, with mainstream publications such as *Newsweek*, *Esquire*, and *The New York Times Magazine* devoting big stories to the film, its director, and its star, Denzel Washington. As with *JFK*,

[22]Simpson, Janice C., "Words With Spike," *Time*, November 23, 1992, p. 66.

[23]Randolph, Laura B., "Denzel Washington and the Making of Malcolm X," *Ebony*, December 1992, p. 128.

[24]Ibid.

Oliver Stone's controversial film on the assassination of John Kennedy, the media coverage of *Malcolm X* did not consist of typical movie reviews, but rather feature stories.

To see the movie is to understand what all the fuss is about. *Malcolm X* is moviemaking on a grand scale. In three hours and twenty minutes—an eternity by Hollywood standards—Lee introduces a political figure to millions of Americans, black and white alike, who know far too little about the man who continues to generate such brand-name recognition twenty-seven years after his death. By tracing Malcolm Little's life from his turbulent childhood to his assassination at age thirty-nine, Lee teaches the audience what it may have forgotten—or, more likely, never knew—about a person who came to symbolize the black man's struggle for equality in a racist society.

Working with cinematographer Ernest Dickerson, Lee depicts Malcolm X's remarkable evolution from Harlem drug peddler and petty thief to a leader of the Nation of Islam, the Muslim religious sect headed by the Honorable Elijah Muhammad (played by Al Freeman Jr.). The turning point in Malcolm's life comes when he does a six-year stint in prison for robbery in the late 1940s. There, he

Passenger 57 (1992): Wesley Snipes

The Secret (TV, 1992): Brock Peters with Kirk Douglas

209

Candyman (1992): Tony Todd

meets Baines (Albert Hall), a fellow inmate who initiates Malcolm's rebirth and eventual induction into the Nation of Islam. When Malcolm Little reemerges from prison, his last name replaced with an X to signify the loss of his African identity during slavery, he becomes a formidable spokesperson for Elijah Muhammad's cause.

Given the nature of that cause—black separatism from the racist "white devils" in America—Malcolm X generates both fear and awe in white people and in less-militant black leaders. But as played by Denzel Washington, he also displays a keen intellect, an embracing sense of humor, and the gift of pointed, uncompromising communications. Eventually, before his assassination at the hands of several Nation of Islam brothers, Malcolm X rejects Elijah Muhammad's racist doctrine and adopts a broader vision of racial unity. As the

movie shows us, that transformation is a part of Malcolm X's legacy, much as his belief in education, responsibility and self-determination are the markers he left for future generations.

Nuns, Executives and Politicians

Nothing could be more of a departure from *Malcolm X* than *Sister Act*, but this lightweight Disney comedy did have one thing in common with Spike Lee's epic: It made a buckets full of money. Starring Whoopi Goldberg, the movie is a contrived but enjoyable romp through a Reno gambling casino and a San Francisco nunnery. It's also a testament to the effectiveness of the old Hollywood formula, which can still work its magic. By year-end, the Disney people had planned a sequel.

The story line of *Sister Act* is remarkably simple. Goldberg plays Deloris Van Cartier, a singer with a bad lounge act and a worse boyfriend, a (white) mobster played by Harvey Keitel. When Deloris witnesses her boyfriend's execution of one of his flunkies, the police decide to hide her in a convent until she can testify. There, she clashes with the Mother Superior (Maggie Smith), who insists that Deloris blend into the convent by wearing a habit and observing their daily rituals.

Deloris has a hard time following this directive, so the Mother Superior decides to keep her out of trouble by having her join the church choir. The women (all white) sing horribly, of course, and Deloris faces the challenge of transforming them into a real choir. This is where the movies has its best moments, as Deloris leads the nuns through her customized renditions of oldies such as "My Guy," which becomes "My God." The movie ends with an obligatory chase scene, in which the bad guys meet the nuns. Needless to say, the nuns prevail.

Say what you will about the content of the movie, but one thing is clear. With an Academy Award for her role in *Ghost*, the success of *Sister Act*, and a new television talk show, Goldberg is America's reigning black female superstar. The *Whoopi* talk show, launched in September 1992, is available to a huge audience through 180 syndicated stations.[25] But it remains to be seen if she

[25]Skow, John, "The Joy of Being Whoopi," *Time*, September 21, 1992, p. 58.

can transfer her stage and screen persona to an interview format. Television is essentially distraction entertainment, after all, and a talk show doesn't have the dramatic and comedic potential of a feature film.

While Goldberg soared in 1992, Eddie Murphy stalled out in *Boomerang,* his first film in two years. The Paramount release was expected to be a huge success but pulled in about $70 million, a relatively paltry figure when compared to the stratospheric sales of Murphy's successful movies in the 1980s. The original *Beverly Hills Cop,* for example, grossed more than $230 million.

In *Boomerang,* which was directed by Reginald Hudlin (of *House Party* fame), Murphy plays Marcus Graham, a successful cosmetics executive and relentless womanizer who gets a taste of his own medicine from Jacqueline (Robin Givens), a fellow executive who treats Marcus with the very disrespect that he dishes out to women. In response, Marcus begins to date a nice woman (Halle Berry) and learns his lessons about how women should be treated.

While *Boomerang* had a few decent reviews—*Newsweek* called it Murphy's best comedy since *48 Hours*[26]—others treated it less kindly. *New York,* for one, said that what Murphy does onscreen "is not a performance but a career move. . . . He looks two-dimensional, almost like a cardboard cutout for his own movie."[27] That sense of detachment has plagued Murphy in several of his recent movies. Murphy does not seem to grow as an actor, and it seems as if he no longer shares the joy of performing with his audience. If he's too bored with his craft to develop his skills and maintain the verve and energy of his early performances, then the audience will become bored as well.

Murphy's box-office appeal will be tested again in *The Distinguished Gentleman,* which was released at the end of 1992. With this comedy, Disney hopes to rework its magic (a la *Sister Act*) by placing a character in an unlikely situation. Here Murphy is Thomas Jefferson Johnson, a small-time con man, and the place is the United States Congress. Johnson wins a seat by mistake and, much to his delight, quickly learns that the payoffs by lobbyists are fast and furious. By the end of the movie, of course, Johnson has developed a conscience.

Profits From the Streets

Two highly profitable movies in 1992 featured rising black artists—Wesley Snipes as the costar of *White Men Can't Jump* and Ernest Dickerson as cowriter and director of *Juice.* In 1991, the two worked together on Spike Lee's *Jungle Fever.*

Mississippi Masala (1992): Denzel Washington with Sarita Choudhoury

[26]Kroll, Jack, "Big Laughs and Cheap Thrills," *Newsweek,* July 6, 1992, p. 54.

[27]Denby, David, "Bad-News Girls," *New York,* July 20, 1992, p. 51.

Snipes starred in the movie and Dickerson served as director of photography, as he has on all of Lee's films including *Malcolm X.*

In *White Men Can't Jump,* Snipes does a star turn that wins him critical acclaim. Playing opposite Woody Harrelson, the slow-witted bartender in the television sitcom "Cheers," Snipes personifies a basketball hustler who works the public courts of Los Angeles. Following this performance, *Newsweek* called Snipes "one of our most versatile young actors," *The New Yorker* described him as "just amazing," and *The Nation* dubbed him "a star down to his toenails."

Snipes had some fine material to work with in *White Men Can't Jump.* Written and directed by Ron Shelton, who made the highly successful *Bull Durham* in 1988, the film focuses on the relationship between Sidney, the slick character played by Snipes, and Billy (Woody Harrelson), a deceptively geeky white ball player adept at hustling himself. When they first meet, in fact, Billy works his standard hustle on Sidney. Laughing goodnaturedly as Sidney's friends call him a chump—he is, after all, a goofy-looking white guy on black turf—Billy proceeds to win $62 from Sidney in a shooting contest.

From there, the movie takes off as Sidney and Billy become partners in hustling, touring the courts of L.A. to fool black street players with a "white guy" routine. You don't have to be a basketball fan to enjoy the action of the street games, and you don't have to be hip to like the rhythm of the language, starting with the inspired battle of "your mother" jokes that opens the movie. While *White Men Can't Jump* may seem slow-moving to those raised on action-thrillers, it offers us an interesting look at male friendship.

White Men Can't Jump grossed more than $34 million in box-office rentals, bringing Snipes's name to an ever-widening audience. And by the end of 1992, his first major film, *Passenger 57,* had been released (see discussion following). But with Snipes at the beginning of his career, one can only hope that he heeds the mistakes of others and focuses on his work, not the trappings of stardom. Given his meteoric rise, Snipes must be careful not to surround himself with yes-men who fail to challenge his choices and help sustain his career.

Like *White Men Can't Jump,* Ernest Dickerson's

Juice was a financial success, albeit on a lower-budget scale. In his first outing as a director, Dickerson tells a coming-of-age story about four friends in Harlem—"Q" (Omar Epps), Bishop (Tupak Shakur), Raheem (Kahlil Kain), and Steel (Jermaine Hopkins). The film falls into the genre of John Singleton's *Boyz N the Hood,* only it is even more grim in its lack of hope that the boys can overcome their environment.

The only one of the four friends with any aspirations is Q, who wants to be a disc jockey. The boys skip school and spend their days aimlessly—hanging out in a pool hall, shoplifting, doing nothing. Dickerson presents this daily routine as an absolute reality—the way things are and always will be. We don't see any ray of hope, and except for Q's modest dream of being a deejay, the boys don't seem to either.

Bishop, for his part, only wants to get "juice," meaning power and respect on the streets. When the boys rob a grocery store one night, Bishop kills the owner for no apparent reason. The boys escape and Raheem argues with Bishop about the shooting. When Raheem tries to take the gun from Bishop, his friend responds with rage. He shoots and kills Raheem, and then coolly maneuvers his way through a police interrogation. By the end of the movie, Bishop also shoots Steel (who lives) and tries to kill Q. As the two struggle, Bishop falls off a rooftop to his death.

Dickerson's story covers some of the same territory as other films set in the inenr city—the violence is pervasive and the route to escape is narrow—but it seems to lack the passion of *Boyz N the Hood* and Matty Rich's *Straight Out of Brooklyn.* Both of those stories had us rooting for their characters, while *Juice* leaves us with an oddly empty feeling.

Mixing It Up in Hollywood

Some of the year's big films paired familiar black actors, such as Danny Glover, Sidney Poitier, and Morgan Freeman, with white performers of equal experience and stature. And two new faces in Hollywood circles, Wesley Snipes and Whitney Houston, also played lead roles in integrated movies designed to appeal to a mixed audience.

Juice (1992): Director
Ernest Dickerson

Juice (1992): From left: Tupac Skakur, Omar Epps, Khalil Kain, and Vincent Laresca

At year-end, the most lucrative of these films was *Lethal Weapon 3*. In the third installment of the congenial Danny Glover/Mel Gibson partnership, LAPD detectives Roger Murtaugh (Glover) and Martin Riggs (Gibson) must bring down an ex-cop who now sells weapons on the streets. Despite its financial success, the movie never gets beyond its tired and violent formula of fights, chase scenes, explosions, killings and other action-packed horrors.

In fact, the violent nonstop action of *Lethal Weapon 3*—much of it carried out by the two LAPD buddies—drew criticism because the movie was released on the heels of the Los Angeles riots in May 1992. The seeds of those riots, of course, were planted by the LAPD's violent beating of Rodney King. While the timing of the two events was coincidental, that didn't stop David Denby of *New York* magazine from declaring that *"Lethal Weapon 3* deserves whatever contempt it gets."[28]

Danny Glover's character, Sergeant Murtaugh, also draws Denby's ire. By *Lethal Weapon 3*, the nearly-retired detective and family man who charmed us in the original *Lethal Weapon* (1987) has become a cartoon character. (Not that Martin Riggs, Gibson's character, fares much better.) But as Denby points out in his review: "Black actors have fought for half a century to escape roles, and performances, like this one. Why is Glover giving up the fight?"

With the September release of *Sneakers*, we got a fresher combination of screen personas. The Universal Pictures film paired Robert Redford and Sidney Poitier as the senior operatives in a shady firm that performs high-tech security checks for corporate clients. Poitier plays Donald Crease, a twenty-two-year CIA veteran who was booted from the agency due to a "personality conflict." Redford's character, Martin Bishop, is on the lam from computer crimes he committed twenty-five years earlier as a college student.

Bishop gets an offer he can't refuse. Two government agents threaten to expose his past unless his company locates a "black box" that the bad guys will use to break into the computer systems of every government agency. Bishop has to marshal

all his resources to pull off the job, including Crease and his three other assistants—Mother (Dan Aykroyd), Carl (River Phoenix), and Whistler (David Strathairn). The quirky group of technical wizards, each with his own brand of breaking-and-entering skills, begins the chase for the box.

What's notable about Poitier's role in the film, though he gives a fine performance, is its relatively small size. *Sneakers* is Poitier's third film since his return to acting on the screen in 1988 following a ten-year absence. In the other two films—*Shoot to Kill* and *Little Nikita*—he had starring roles. But like many who have passed by the prime moviego-

White Men Can't Jump (1992): Wesley Snipes with Woody Harrelson

---

[28]Denby, David, "Idiot's Delight," *New York*, June 1, 1992, p. 56.

ing age groups, Poitier becomes part of an ensemble cast in *Sneakers* that can appeal to younger viewers.

Nonetheless, Poitier is still one of our most charismatic actors, and he will no doubt be in demand for the rest of his life. Unlike many who achieve sudden fame and then fizzle from sight, Poitier has worked for four decades as an actor (in forty-three films), director, and producer. For his distinctive body of work on the screen, the American Film Institute presented Poitier its 1992 Lifetime Achievement Award.

Like Poitier, Morgan Freeman had a relatively

small role in *Unforgiven*, Clint Eastwood's 1992 film that was critically acclaimed for its realistic depiction of the Wild—and often violent—West. But Freeman has made a career of delivering excellent performances in primarily character roles, and his work in *Unforgiven* is no exception.

Freeman plays Ned Logan, the former gunslinging comrade of Will Munny (Eastwood) who joins him in a bounty hunt for two cowboys who cut a prostitute's face. If Munny and Logan kill the boys, they will collect $1,000 from the prostitutes who posted the bounty. The women resent the light-handed justice that the town sheriff (Gene Hackman) has doled out to the boys, so they have taken matters into their own hands. But the question is, do two aging gunslingers still have what it takes to end another man's life?

Freeman's character serves as the only reflective, or moralistic, voice in the movie. When Munny and Logan finally track down the boys, Logan realizes that he cannot kill them. Munny pulls the trigger himself. Later, Logan refuses to reveal his partner's whereabouts to the sheriff, who then beats him to death. It is ironic that the one moral character in the story—who chooses not to shoot another human being for money—comes to such a violent end.

The big Hollywood movies of 1992 also featured some rising black artists, most notably Wesley Snipes in *Passenger 57*. The movie opened in November on nearly two thousand screens across the United States and Canada, a tremendous level of exposure afforded only to the major studios' blockbuster hopefuls, such as *Home Alone 2, The Bodyguard,* and *The Distinguished Gentleman*. The film is also notable in that it was directed by Kevin Hooks, a black actor who made his big screen directorial debut in 1991 with *Strictly Business*. (His father, veteran actor Robert Hooks, has a part in the movie too).

For Snipes, whose prior four films reached a smaller audience, *Passenger 57* was the leap into the big times. He stars as John Cutter, an airline antiterrorist expert who must outwit Charles Rane (Bruce Payne), a vicious but intelligent villain who hijacks a plane that is taking him to Los Angeles, where he will stand trial for past crimes. Cutter, who is on the plane, enlists the help of a stewardess (Alex Datcher) and his buddy on the ground (Tom

Sizemore), whom he manages to contact by telephone.

But what starts as a good concept falls a bit flat. The movie loses some of its tension when the hijackers force a landing in a small airport and Cutter leaves the plane. He must spend time fighting with local authorities—who believe he's the hijacker, no the airline's head of security—before he can return to his mission of bringing in Rane and saving the passengers. The movie stretches the limits of plausibility when the hijackers pass on their chance to escape and instead chase Cutter around a carnival, trying to kill him.

Despite the glitches in the story line, the pairing of Snipes with Bruce Payne, a British actor who played the devil in Warner Bros.' *Switch*, seemed to offer the right chemistry of good against evil. And Snipes, for his part, has an innate style and star quality that filled the screen. Now he faces the challenge of building on his 1992 successes— *White Men Can't Jump, Passenger 57,* and *Waterdance,* a small but critically-acclaimed film—with roles that will fuel his career for the long run.

The same might be said of Whitney Houston, who made her screen debut in *The Bodyguard,* a Warners picture starring Kevin Costner. She plays Rachel Maron, a popular singer with a budding acting career who begins to receive death threats. Frank Farmer (Costner) becomes her bodyguard, and the inevitable happens: they fall in love.

The movie, which grossed a whopping $52.9 million by year's end, was obviously designed for a mass audience. Costner has had the Midas Touch in recent years with films such as *Dances With Wolves, JFK,* and *Robin Hood: Prince of Thieves.* And Houston, while an unknown in the movie business, has a ready-made audience among her music fans. Interestingly, however, the film didn't trust the audience to accept a fully developed sexual relationship between a white man and black woman. Some of the steamy love scenes originally filmed were edited out for fear that they would not go over well in the mainstream.

Damon Wayans (of *In Living Color* fame) also starred in his second feature film in 1992, *Mo'*

Sneakers (1992): Sidney Poitier with David Strathairn, Dan Aykroyd, River Phoenix, and Robert Redford

The Bodyguard (1992): Whitney Houston with Kevin Costner

The Bodyguard (1992): Whitney Houston

Money. His screen debut with Bruce Willis in *The Last Boy Scout* proved to be a big hit. But this time around Wayans also wrote and produced the film, which was relatively successful as a first production.

In *Mo' Money,* Wayans plays Johnny Stewart, a street con artist who gets an honest job at a credit card company after an encounter with the police. But he soon becomes involved in a big credit card scam that is far removed from the small scale hustling he did on the streets. Johnny not only gets himself out of this mess, but he also gets the girl, an executive played by Stacey Dash. While the movie is predictable, Wayans gets a chance to display his comedic skill, which was honed on his successful TV series.

Independent Efforts

Two small independent films, both of which made less than $10 million at the box office, were successful in their own right. *Mississippi Masala,*

218

Mo' Money (1992): Damon Wayans and Marlon Wayans

directed by Mira Nair (who made *Salaam Bombay!*), focuses on a culture clash in a small southern town. This clash is depicted by two families, one a group of displaced Indians who were forced to leave Uganda in the early 1970s by Idi Amin's regime, and the other a black American family with a belief in virtues of hard word.

The movie follows the love story between Mina (Sarita Choudhury), a young Indian woman who cleans bathrooms in the roadside motel operated by her extended family, and Demetrius (Denzel Washington), a black man who runs his own carpet-cleaning business. When the news of their affair gets out, each must deal with the consequences. Mina's family disapproves strongly of her black lover; Demetrius loses his bank loan when he is jailed for fighting with Mina's cousin. In the end, their solution is to leave town together to rebuild Demetrius' business.

Another independent film, *Daughters of the Dust*, is an unusual movie in many ways—its subject, its style and its focus on black women. In

Mo' Money (1992): Damon Wayans
and Stacey Dash

her first feature-length film, writer/director Julie Dash focuses on an African family in 1902 who inhabit the Sea Islands, located off the coast of Georgia. The "Gullah" family holds a reunion just before they are to move to the mainland, breaking their ties with tradition and joining the modern world.

Dash's movie is beautifully filmed—it won an award for best cinematography at the Sundance Film Festival—but the pace is painfully slow by today's standards. While it takes some patience

Malcolm X (1992): Angela Bassett and Denzel Washington

Malcolm X (1992): Director, coproducer, and writer Spike Lee

and alertness to follow the story, *Daughters of the Dust* does explore a forgotten segment of America society that one is unlikely to see elsewhere.

Another 1992 film which enjoyed moderate success was TriStar's essay into Stephen King field, a horror movie called *Candyman*. Bernard Rose both wrote and directed this thriller from a Clive Barker original story. In it Tony Todd gave a frightening performance as a hook-handed specter, killing to perpetuate his own existance.

The kind of success enjoyed by these new films of the late eighties and thus far into the nineties may be pegged as a turning point in film history. If the Hollywood establishment maintains that momentum (when some fifteen hundred movie screens in the United States and Canada were showing black oriented films) rather than considering the current interest in black films only a passing fancy, we can expect these and other similar ones about issues of importance to the black community to become a part of our mainstream consciousness.

Malcolm X (1992): Denzel Washington

Unforgiven (1992): Morgan Freeman

ORDER NOW!
More Citadel Film Books

If you like this book, you'll love the other titles in the award-winning Citadel Film Series. From James Stewart to Moe Howard and The Three Stooges, Woody Allen to John Wayne, The Citadel Film Series is America's largest and oldest film book library.

With more than 150 titles--and more on the way!--Citadel Film Books make perfect gifts for a loved one, a friend, or best of all, yourself!

A complete listing of the Citadel Film Series appears below.
If you know what books you want, why not order now!
It's easy! Just call 1-800-447-BOOK and have your MasterCard or Visa ready.

STARS
Alan Ladd
Barbra Streisand: First Decade
Barbra Streisand: Second
  Decade
Bela Lugosi
Bette Davis
Boris Karloff
The Bowery Boys
Buster Keaton
Carole Lombard
Cary Grant
Charles Bronson
Charlie Chaplin
Clark Gable
Clint Eastwood
Curly
Dustin Hoffman
Edward G. Robinson
Elizabeth Taylor
Elvis Presley
Errol Flynn
Frank Sinatra
Gary Cooper
Gene Kelly
Gina Lollobrigida
Gloria Swanson
Gregory Peck
Greta Garbo
Henry Fonda
Humphrey Bogart
Ingrid Bergman
Jack Lemmon
Jack Nicholson
James Cagney
James Dean: Behind the Scene
Jane Fonda
Jeanette MacDonald & Nelson
  Eddy
Joan Crawford

John Wayne Films
John Wayne Reference Book
John Wayne Scrapbook
Judy Garland
Katharine Hepburn
Kirk Douglas
Laurel & Hardy
Lauren Bacall
Laurence Olivier
Mae West
Marilyn Monroe
Marlene Dietrich
Marlon Brando
Marx Brothers
Moe Howard & the Three
  Stooges
Norma Shearer
Olivia de Havilland
Orson Welles
Paul Newman
Peter Lorre
Rita Hayworth
Robert De Niro
Robert Redford
Sean Connery
Sexbomb: Jayne Mansfield
Shirley MacLaine
Shirley Temple
The Sinatra Scrapbook
Spencer Tracy
Steve McQueen
Three Stooges Scrapbook
Warren Beatty
W.C. Fields
William Holden
William Powell
A Wonderful Life: James Stewart
DIRECTORS
Alfred Hitchcock
Cecil B. DeMille

Federico Fellini
Frank Capra
John Ford
John Huston
Woody Allen
GENRE
Bad Guys
Black Hollywood
Black Hollywood: From 1970 to
  Today
Classics of the Gangster Film
Classics of the Horror Film
Divine Images: Jesus on Screen
Early Classics of Foreign Film
Great French Films
Great German Films
Great Romantic Films
Great Science Fiction Films
Harry Warren & the Hollywood
  Musical
Hispanic Hollywood: The Latins
  in Motion Pictures
The Hollywood Western
The Incredible World of 007
The Jewish Image in American
  Film
The Lavender Screen: The Gay
  and Lesbian Films
Martial Arts Movies
The Modern Horror Film
More Classics of the Horror Film
Movie Psychos & Madmen
Our Huckleberry Friend: Johnny
  Mercer
Second Feature: "B" Films
They Sang! They Danced! They
  Romanced!: Hollywood
  Musicals
Thrillers
The West That Never Was

Words and Shadows: Literature
  on the Screen
DECADE
Classics of the Silent Screen
Films of the Twenties
Films of the Thirties
More Films of the 30's
Films of the Forties
Films of the Fifties
Lost Films of the 50's
Films of the Sixties
Films of the Seventies
Films of the Eighties
SPECIAL INTEREST
America on the Rerun
Bugsy (Illustrated screenplay)
Comic Support
Dick Tracy
Favorite Families of TV
Film Flubs
Film Flubs: The Sequel
First Films
Forgotten Films to Remember
Hollywood Cheesecake
Hollywood's Hollywood
Howard Hughes in Hollywood
More Character People
The Nightmare Never Ends:
  Freddy Krueger & "A Night-
  mare on Elm Street"
The "Northern Exposure" Book
The "Quantum Leap" Book
Sex In the Movies
Sherlock Holmes
Son of Film Flubs
Those Glorious Glamour Years
Who Is That?: Familiar Faces and
  Forgotten Names
"You Ain't Heard Nothin' Yet!"

For a free full-color brochure describing the Citadel Film Series in depth, call 1-800-447-BOOK; or send your name and address to Citadel Film Books, Dept. 1216, 120 Enterprise Ave., Secaucus, NJ 07094.